THE BIG
100

JEREMY KOURDI

THE BIG

100

THE 100 BUSINESS
TOOLS YOU NEED
TO SUCCEED

JEREMY KOURDI

Acknowledgements

This book is inspired by many people. First, thanks are due to the business thinkers who have researched, reflected, discovered and developed the practical insights that are explained in this book. Business is a positive, progressive and practical enterprise, and this book is designed to benefit and support anyone pursuing a career in this vital area. Business thinkers and leaders ensure our prosperity and employment; their work enriches our lives; they stimulate, develop and challenge us, and they help us go further than ever before. They are too often pilloried for their occasional shortcomings while their intelligence, originality and success are too rarely acknowledged.

On a much more personal note I owe a huge debt to all my clients and colleagues who have, without doubt, provided the most interesting and exciting environment in which to work, learn and develop. Particular thanks are due to my friend and colleague Brian Edwards: an inspiring coach, a talented leader, and a constant source of clarity, insight and support.

I am also very grateful to Julie Kourdi who has worked as researcher and editor with great intelligence and tireless skill, expertise and good humour. She has been a constant source of help and sound advice.

Finally, thanks are due to the talented publishing team at Hodder & Stoughton whose patience and expertise is much appreciated.

I hope that these ideas will provide you with the inspiration to find out more and stimulate your thinking along new, creative lines, generating brilliant ideas for the future.

Jeremy Kourdi

Contents

Developing innovation and creativity

Developing people, organizations and culture

Introduction

What is the key to success in business for individuals, managers and organizations? Many answers come to mind, notably the ability to serve customers by providing great products or service and creating value, and to do this in way that is efficient, competitive, profitable and valued. Meeting this challenge, however, requires a range of leadership skills, including: the ability to innovate, to learn and develop; to get the best from the people, knowledge and resources around you; and to build business relationships inside and outside the organization. And if all this were not difficult enough, these things need to be achieved constantly, while expectations, opportunities and challenges are constantly shifting. Now, more than ever, is a time of complexity, volatility and change.

New ideas, energy and the ability to fit new contexts and meet new challenges are therefore needed constantly to ensure success. That is why business tools and techniques are so valuable – because they help us meet the many varied challenges faced by business managers and leaders. This is a book about some of the best tools and techniques used in business. What unites these business ideas is their proven power and potency. They are not only insightful and useful but they have worked – and often brilliantly or despite great adversity. The ability of the people who conceived and applied these ideas should be applauded.

Interestingly, there are several different themes that run through many of these ideas. These include a willingness to experiment and take a risk, coupled with an ability to understand the root causes of an issue and do something distinctive. Simplicity and an understanding of the need to be practical and implement the idea are also common features of these techniques. Some ideas seem to confirm Peter Drucker's point that great ideas and decisions are a blend of rigorous analysis and intuition. Finally, the need to be practical, follow through and ensure success is shown by the recurring need to monitor, measure and refine the way the idea works.

There are several specific qualities that characterize the ideas in this book. Keeping these in mind will help you succeed with each technique by applying it successfully to your own context.

In particular, the likelihood of success increases if you:

- engage people with the technique wherever possible and appropriate
- be clear about the specific challenge, issue or opportunity that is being addressed
- question and constantly challenge assumptions: yours and others'
- develop a mindset that looks for ways to learn and improve, and are ready to confront challenges and problems early
- understand that good ideas can come from anywhere
- follow through – be practical and realistic, and plan implementation
- give people praise and credit, thereby building momentum
- work tirelessly to remove constraints, fears and inhibitions
- balance intuition and analysis
- build collaboration and teamwork
- avoid the pitfalls of decision-making (see technique number 86)
- be self-aware and develop your skills.

Remember: energy, flexibility, creativity and ingenuity are vital, and there is no room for complacency and little tolerance for inefficiency.

I hope that these ideas will help you with your work and stimulate your thinking along new, creative lines, generating brilliant ideas for the future.

Jeremy Kourdi

LEADERSHIP AND CHANGE

THE GROW MODEL FOR COACHING

The single most important technique for executive coaching

The GROW model, developed by Sir John Whitmore, provides a framework for coaching. GROW has four stages: Goals, Reality, Options and Way forward. Responsibility for setting goals rests with the coachee. The coach works in a non-directive way, supporting and challenging.

Goals

This focuses on the coachee's aims and priorities. It sets the agenda for the coaching conversation. The coach should be flexible and prepared to explore, question and challenge. This is achieved with questioning and empathy. The outcome is a clear set of goals for the session and the overall coaching relationship.

Questions include:

- What is your goal?
- What are your priorities?
- What are you trying to achieve?
- How will you know when you have achieved it?
- Is the goal specific and measurable?
- How will you know when it has been achieved?
- What will success look like?

Reality

Explore the learner's current position: the reality of their circumstances and their concerns relating to their goals. The coach needs to help the coachee analyse and understand the significant issues relating to their goal through intelligent questioning. The coach can also provide information and summarize the situation to clarify the reality.

Questions include:

- Can you control the result? What don't you have control over?
- What are the milestones or key points to achieving goals?
- Who is involved and what effect could they have?
- What have you done so far, and what are the results?
- What are the major issues you are encountering?

Options

The coach helps the coachee to generate options, strategies and action plans for achieving goals. This can uncover new aspects of the individual's current position with the result that discussion reverts back to the coachee's reality. This is fine if it is productive or enlightening – the aim is to help the individual, not rigidly follow a process.

Questions include:

- What options do you have? Which do you favour and why?
- If you had unlimited resources, what options would you have?
- Could you link your goal to another organizational issue?
- What would be the perfect solution?

Way forward

Do not rush the final stage. The aim is to agree what needs to be done. It can help for the coachee to develop a practical plan to implement their option. The coach should be a sounding board, highlighting strengths and weaknesses, testing the approach and offering additional perspectives.

Questions include:

- What are you going to do – and when? Who needs to know? What support and resources do you need?
- How will you overcome obstacles and ensure success?

Finally, the most effective plans incorporate a review and feedback process to check progress and provide motivation.

DEVELOPING INFLUENCE AND ASSERTIVE LEADERSHIP

Providing support and challenge while strengthening results and relationships

Whether you are giving feedback or selling a product or an idea, influencing requires an understanding of how your behaviour affects others.

Overview

All individuals have their own personality – the result both of nature and nurture – and this remains largely unchanging. However, behaviour is different: it is flexible and capable of being developed and enhanced. It's useful to consider behaviour (yours and others) in terms of warmth or coldness, dominance or submissiveness.

- **Warm** means being supportive, open, positive, empathetic, constructive and engaging – not simply 'friendly'.
- **Cold** means being suspicious, detached, not focused on people or relationships.
- **Dominant** means being challenging, in control, confident, strong, authoritative and direct.
- **Submissive** means subduing your own thoughts or actions for something or someone else.

The diagram below (the assertiveness model) highlights different types of behaviour (based on the Thomas-Kilmann Conflict Mode Instrument).

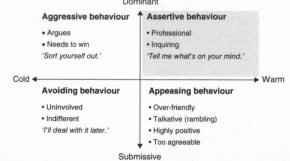

Aggressive: dominant and cold behaviour

When dealing with aggressive behaviour, the best approach is to:

- increase your dominance to match their high dominance levels
- ensure that you are demonstrating behaviour that is assertive and warm rather than aggressive
- use open questions to generate understanding
- use body language and tone of voice to increase your dominance levels.

Avoiding: cold and submissive behaviour

When dealing with avoiding behaviour, the first priority is to get people engaged. Useful techniques include displaying lower dominance and higher warmth, using open questions aimed at making them feel secure and softening body language and intonation while continuing to smile.

Appeasing: warm and submissive behaviour

When dealing with appeasing individuals, it can help to:

- stay focused to keep them on track
- use open questions that appeal to their social needs but temper these with closed questions when they waffle
- ask summary questions to maintain clarity and focus
- use their name if you are interrupting them.

Assertive: warm and dominant behaviour

When dealing with conflict, it can help to be assertive and encourage others to be assertive as well. Consider how easy it is to warm up behaviour: why and when is it not easy? Why do we, as individuals, not behave in an assertive manner? What is it that hinders supportive and challenging behaviour? Finally, what are the most important questions for you to ask?

VISIONING

Creating your future

By imagining the future you want and then translating those ideas into practical and actionable plans, you will make it happen.

Orienting thinking towards the future is particularly important for middle and senior managers and leaders because it provides focus, determines the company's culture, builds resilience and adaptability and engages employees.

The need

A powerful vision motivates and guides everyone at all levels in a company. People manage what is in front of them, as daily and short-term tasks understandably dominate our routine and thinking. This certainly keeps things running smoothly in the stable present but is ill suited to coping with change or taking advantage of (or creating) opportunities. Visioning liberates us from simply managing the present, achieving more of the same or being unprepared for new developments, and thus enables us to build a more successful future.

The process

Visioning involves assessing and challenging current thinking and methods, developing new ideas and deciding on the future you would like. It is also necessary to look outside your company – noticing and understanding trends, identifying threats and opportunities.

It can be helpful to involve others in a visioning exercise by asking their views on various issues. These questions will prompt thinking and encourage each person to consider and challenge the company's aims and activities and to suggest new options (giving reasons for their choices).

Using these answers, you identify the most common issues and ideas, reduce these options to the ones that are most significant and then draft a provisional vision statement – this can be done by a smaller group of people, with the final vision being reviewed and approved by everyone involved. As well as generating ideas and opening up discussions, a major advantage of involving others in the visioning process is that you will gain their commitment to the final vision.

Once you have developed your vision, determine how it can be achieved:

- Deal with any barriers that may stand in the way and consider how future events may affect it.
- Develop a practical plan and communicate the vision and plan to everyone – show people why it is important, what it will achieve and how it will work and gain their commitment.
- To bring others with you, your vision needs to be clear, convincing, credible, easy to grasp, actionable, inspiring and focused – but not overly prescriptive, to provide flexibility and adaptability.

What's next?

A vision is for nothing if it is not acted upon. You should ensure that all strategy and decisions are guided by the vision and that everyone remains committed to the vision. A vision also needs to be reviewed and adapted to changing circumstances to ensure that it remains relevant and useful.

THE CHANGE CURVE

Understanding how people respond to change

The human reaction to change is now well understood. The change process is commonly understood by reference to the research on people's reaction to bereavement. Elisabeth Kübler-Ross has been a great contributor to our understanding of the experience of loss and bereavement, as well as how we react to changes more generally. The stages of loss that people typically go through are now commonly known as the Change Curve.

Overview

Organizations often refer to the Change Curve in the context of job loss and redundancy. Dr Kübler-Ross undertook her research on dying by interviewing terminally ill patients. Although this is one of the most extreme and disturbing changes that anyone can face, the reactions to it are the same as for many different types of change. There are several key stages that people go through, as shown in the graph below:

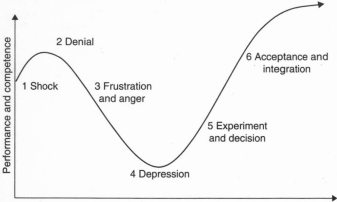

1 **Shock.** The first reaction can often be shock – and all the emotion that results from this.

2 **Denial.** This is a typical reaction and it is important and necessary. It helps cushion the impact of the inevitability of change.

3 **Frustration and anger.** The person resents the change that they must face while others are less affected.

4 **Depression.** First, the person feels deep disappointment, perhaps a sense of personal failing, things not done, wrongs committed. Around this time they may also engage in *bargaining*: beginning to accept the change but striking bargains –for more time, for example,.

5 **Experiment and decision.** Initial engagement with the new situation and learning how to work in the new situation, as well as making choices and decisions, and regaining control.

6 **Acceptance and integration.** Dr Kübler-Ross describes this stage as neither happy nor unhappy. While it is devoid of feelings, it is not resignation – it is really a victory.

People who are made redundant can go through a similar process. Just as with other types of change, people often go through a first stage before denial – that of shock or disbelief. We have witnessed people in shock following news of their redundancy. It can take a long time for people to reach the acceptance stage and often people oscillate between the different stages.

THE LEADERSHIP PIPELINE

Developing a leader-powered business

Performance is inseparable from a company's approach to leadership development. Developed by Ram Charan, Stephen Drotter and James Noel, the Leadership Pipeline is a company-wide framework for developing future managers and leaders.

Overview

The Leadership Pipeline is a continual process that ensures a throughput of talented leaders. It is a practical, easily understood system that clearly explains what is required to work successfully at each leadership level, helping:

- individuals and companies to understand what is required for excellence at each level
- individuals to develop their skills, optimize potential and progress their careers
- organizations to manage and develop talent, and to build strategic and organizational capabilities.

How it works

The Leadership Pipeline represents the flow of internal talent into business-critical roles. As such, organizational structures, processes and reward mechanisms are geared towards encouraging preferred behaviours. For the individual, the Pipeline clarifies the development path that will build the leadership capabilities required to operate successfully at higher levels. At each stage:

- people need to be clear about the capabilities needed for each level
- managers and leaders should use the skills and values that are expected at each level so that others can operate effectively.

Traditional approaches to leadership development tend to simply strengthen existing skills, and inadequate attention is paid to learning new ones.

The Leadership Pipeline formally recognizes that change and improved performance occur best when the skills that are needed for the next level are built on a solid foundation at previous levels and when individuals are given the time and correct support and training to learn the skills, time management and values required for the new role.

This clear framework makes it easy for people to see what capabilities and values are needed for successful career progression and it focuses people on the skills the organization needs – thus improving both current and future performance.

Working towards successful transitions

Typically, career progression involves making successful transitions at six key stages:

1 From managing yourself to managing others
2 From managing others to managing managers
3 From managing managers to functional director
4 From functional director to business director
5 From business director to group business director
6 From group business director to company director.

In reality, people often make these transitions with little support and inadequate preparation, commonly modelling themselves on their predecessors and learning what works through trial and error. The Leadership Pipeline makes explicit what is required for success at each level. In particular, it clarifies the requirements in three key areas:

1 Developing new skills
2 Improving time management
3 Adopting the values the organization is looking for.

Acquiring these capabilities at each level builds the foundation for success at the next level. Consequently, this focus on skills, time management and values prioritizes improved performance for advancement – benefiting both the individual and the company.

EMPLOYEE ENGAGEMENT AND THE THREE-FACTOR THEORY

The three things that matter most to people at work

The factors that influence employee engagement combine in different ways and at different times for each person. Obviously, pay and leadership are important – with a direct relationship between pay and effort and the quality of leadership being critical to employee engagement. In addition, people like to do work that has meaning and purpose.

Following international research, Sirota Consulting developed the Three-Factor Theory, addressing employee engagement by addressing three basic needs: equity, achievement and camaraderie.

Leaders need to engage, inspire and energize their people. Gaining commitment and getting people to acquire new skills and achieve their full potential leads to ongoing improvements in performance, benefiting all concerned – individuals, teams and companies. The Three Factor Theory establishes a self-sustaining cycle of effective employee engagement by ensuring that practices and policies focus on equity, achievement and camaraderie.

Equity

People need to feel they are being treated fairly – especially in relation to others both inside and outside the company. This includes:

- **physical** aspects – for example, working in a safe environment and being physically able to do a job
- **economic** factors – people need to feel that their pay, benefits and job security are fair
- **psychological** issues – including being treated with respect and consideration.

Achievement

People work better and achieve more if they believe in what they are doing and have confidence in the direction they are going. In short, they work best when they feel they are achieving something. Six issues influence this:

1 Having challenging work and being able to use their skills
2 Having the opportunity to develop their capabilities and to take risks
3 Having the resources, authority, information and support to work effectively
4 Knowing that the work is important and has value and purpose
5 Receiving recognition – both financial and non-financial
6 Having pride in the company's aims, ethics, products and brand values.

Camaraderie

It is important for individuals to have good relations with co-workers. This requires congenial, co-operative, interesting and supportive relationships at all levels, with the most immediate ones being the most significant. This involves relationships:

- with co-workers
- within the business unit
- across on-site departments
- across the whole company.

THE NINE PRINCIPLES
OF MOTIVATION

Creating the right environment

So much in business depends on motivating others. There is only so much any one person can do, so getting the most out of others is crucial to success. This all begins with winning trust – everything else follows.

Motivating others is an essential part of leadership. Your ability to motivate others relies on what they think of you and how they think you view them. This requires planning and vigilance and knowing that different people are motivated by different things. To motivate effectively, you need to know what motivates each person, the pressures they face, what influences their decisions and thinking, and how you can make a difference. These nine principles of motivation will help you to help your colleagues.

1 Be motivated yourself

Self-motivation rallies others. People will 'step up to the plate' if you do so yourself. Knowing what motivates you will help you to motivate others.

2 Recruit people who are highly motivated and assign them to the right position

Match people's motivation to their job. Some are motivated by making sales while others are motivated by following processes, building teams or pursuing new ideas.

3 Treat people as individuals

We all have different values and personalities. What works for one may not motivate another. So, tap into what motivates each individual to improve performance.

4 Set challenging but realistic targets

Nothing is more demotivating than unachievable targets. Nothing is more motivating than achievable, we-can-beat-the-competition targets – they tap into our competitiveness and desire to produce something to be proud of.

5 Focus on progress – it motivates

Everyone responds to a pat on the back – they've earned it and deserve it, so make it happen. The result: an upward spiral of people wanting to achieve more.

6 Develop an environment that motivates people

Eliminate or minimize anything that blocks motivation – from bureaucracy and unnecessary procedures to lack of resources. Provide training and coaching to develop skills and to make people feel valued.

7 Ensure that people receive fair rewards

Promotion, pay rises, sales commission, profit share, work benefits, additional responsibilities: these motivate people. They give people a reason to stay and to help your company excel.

8 Recognize people's work

We all want our efforts to be acknowledged. Recognition is needed to maintain commitment.

9 Be honest about your intent

Honesty lies at the heart of motivation. Be clear about what your intentions are. People will be motivated only by those they can trust.

SITUATIONAL LEADERSHIP (LEADERSHIP STYLES)

Adapting your approach

Situational leadership improves your ability to lead others and to respond effectively to situations.

Different leadership styles

By adjusting your style to match each challenge, you are more likely to achieve your desired outcome. To decide which approach is best, you need to consider the issues, what needs to happen and the people involved. To develop your situational leadership, you must be self-aware and understand your own style and how it impacts others.

The model of situational leadership developed by Ken Blanchard and Spencer Johnson identifies and details the different leadership styles.

Leadership style	Characteristics
Directing ... telling	**Centres on structure, control and supervision and one-way communication** Effective for teams that are new, temporary or forming A hands-on, decisive and involved approach that directs and emphasizes tasks and deadlines
Coaching ... engaging	**Focuses on directing and supporting – using teaching and guiding skills** Works well with teams that have worked together for a period of time Promotes a balance between short-term and long-term needs – such as monitoring target achievement while developing longer-term priorities

Leadership style	Characteristics
Supporting ... developing	**Involves praising, listening and facilitating development**
	Appropriate for teams that continue to function well
	Leaders are no longer involved in short-term performance and operational measures
	Long-term aspects are more important, with a focus on individual and team development, planning and innovation
Delegating ... hands-off ... facilitating	**Responsibility for routine decisions is handed over**
	Works best with a highly experienced, successful team when little involvement is needed
	The focus is on working externally for the team by developing networks, securing resources and sharing best practice
	Intervention is usually at the request of the team wanting support and advice with defining problems, devising solutions or handling problems

Using the right style

Each situation should use the most appropriate style. For example, directing is useful in exceptional circumstances such as a crisis requiring people to follow a particular course of action or when handling difficult personnel issues.

To decide which style is appropriate, assess the competence, ability, confidence and motivation of those involved. For example:

- Low confidence may indicate reduced commitment, so a supportive and encouraging style is appropriate.
- Low motivation requires a listening approach, to identify the causes and change the situation.

THE JOHN WHITMORE MODEL

Are you setting the right goals in the right way?

Sir John Whitmore gave us the GROW model for coaching and he also highlighted a model for goal-setting that is SMART, PURE and CLEAR, ensuring that you and your colleagues have goals that are appropriate, achievable and successful.

Goal-setting is vital whenever you need to focus someone (including yourself) on a specific objective or series of objectives – for example, at an annual appraisal, when someone starts a new role, or simply at the start of a new project.

When developing people, it is important to provide a focus for action and to ensure a sense of purpose. This is the value of the John Whitmore model: it provides a checklist for goal-setting. So, when you are goal-setting, keep it simple and check that each goal meets the 14 criteria in Whitmore's model.

Specific	**The right goal**	**C**hallenging
Measurable	**P**ositively stated	**L**egal
Attainable	**U**nderstood	**E**nvironmentally sound
Realistic/**R**ealistic	**R**elevant	**A**greed
Time-constrained	**E**thical	**R**ecorded

When goal-setting, distinguish between end goals and performance goals:

- **End goals** are the ultimate objective. They could typically be to gain pro-motion or additional responsibility or to complete a major project (e.g. 'I need to achieve sales of £300,000 this year').
- **Performance goals** establish the level of performance that will help an individual to achieve their end goal. Performance goals include such

elements as quality standards, time management and production targets (e.g. 'I need to develop my negotiating skills').

Think about a current goal you have or one you want to address in the future. Answer the following questions to assess the robustness of your approach to goal setting, monitoring and achievement. Also, comment on how you could improve your approach.

- What is your goal?
- Is it specific? What, exactly, will success look like? Is it an end goal or a performance goal?
- Is it measurable? How will progress be measured and monitored?
- Is it attainable? Do you have the skills and resources needed?
- How will you succeed and what will you do? What could go wrong? What are the risks?
- Is it realistic? How does it relate to other people and activities? Are these links understood and could this goal benefit from other activities or expertise elsewhere in the organization?
- What is the timescale? Are there milestones or dependencies in the plan?
- Is the goal stated as positively as possible, in a way that will engage and encourage people?
- Is it understood – is there a clear vision and view of what success will look like?
- Is it relevant – how well does it relate to other issues and priorities?
- Is it ethical?
- Will it provide the right level of challenge?
- Is it legal and are there legal (or regulatory) issues to consider?
- Is it environmentally sound?
- Is everyone agreed or is more agreement needed?
- Has the goal been recorded and is it being monitored, with progress assessed and lessons learned?

ACTION-CENTRED LEADERSHIP

Managing the task, team and individual

John Adair's Action-Centred Leadership model views the role of leaders as integrating three areas: ensuring that the task, the team and the individual are working effectively and that their needs are met. Success relies on ensuring that all three responsibilities are mutually reinforcing.

Overview

As a leader, people look to you to set the direction, to support them, to help them achieve their goals, to ensure that team members work well together and to make sure that the structures and procedures are in place (and working effectively). It is not enough to have a great idea; you are responsible for making it happen. In short, leadership is a total activity. If individuals aren't motivated, teams will not function well; if teams don't work well, tasks will fail and individual satisfaction falls, and so on. Whether you are leading one team, a business unit or an entire company, you need to provide for:

- **the needs of the task** – provide the appropriate systems, procedures and structures
- **the needs of the team** – promote team cohesiveness so that team members work well together
- **the needs of the individual** – engage each person (by considering pay, their sense of purpose, their need to have achievements and contributions recognized, and their need for status and to be part of something that matters).

A functional approach to leadership

To provide for the needs of the task, team and individuals, John Adair outlines eight leadership functions:

1 **Define the task.** Everyone needs to understand what is expected, so be clear about the task at hand – make it SMART (Specific, Measurable, Attainable, Realistic and Time-constrained).

2 **Plan.** Identify options, look for alternatives, make contingency plans and test your ideas. Working with others in a positive, open-minded, constructive and creative way will help you to develop the best plan.

3 **Brief others.** To create the right conditions and bring people with you, you have to keep people informed. Both teams and individuals will work well only if they have access to information and your thinking – without open communication, confusion or even distrust can seriously hamper business strategy.

4 **Control effectively.** You need self-control and you need to positively control others. Put the right procedures and monitoring in place, delegate tasks and trust others to both take responsibility and deliver results.

5 **Evaluate.** Assess likely consequences, measure and judge the performance of both teams and individuals and provide necessary feedback and training.

6 **Motivate.** Motivate yourself – if you are not motivated, it will be difficult to motivate others. Recruit people who are highly motivated. Set realistic and achievable targets – people respond to doable goals. Focus on progress, reward success and recognize achievements.

7 **Be organized.** Be organized yourself and ensure that teams and individuals have the necessary skills, procedures, structures and resources in place for them to do their jobs efficiently.

8 **Set the right example.** The example you set to others influences their behaviour, motivation and willingness to follow you.

THE SIX STEPS OF DELEGATION

Developmental, productive – the cornerstone of leadership

Without delegation, leaders cannot lead and managers cannot manage. Delegation develops skills, challenges and retains great people, and increases productivity. Yet many people have difficulty delegating. These six steps will help you to delegate effectively.

Delegation requires empowerment and trust. You need to empower people, give them the skills and confidence to act and take risks. You need to trust them and accept that mistakes will happen – mistakes that can be rectified and learned from and that are more than made up for by the progress that is achieved. Delegation is essential precisely because it goes directly to the bottom line – it has a huge impact on productivity, innovation and employee engagement and retention.

Delegation can be learned but, to be successful, it rests entirely on having the right mindset. It is about bringing people with you. While experience helps, what is more important is attitude, good communication skills and confidence in yourself. These six stages provide a framework to help you delegate successfully:

1 Prepare to delegate

Know what you want to achieve. Be clear about goals and priorities and decide how these can be achieved. Plan what needs to happen, and when, and bring people along with you. Winning hearts and minds and making sure people know the reasons for your plan and what is expected of them are essential.

2 Match the person to the task

Know your people. Understand what they can do, their potential, what would challenge and stimulate them. It also helps to understand their future career plans. Make the most of each person's abilities. Look for potential and take risks. With encouragement, training and trust, you will get more from each person.

3 Discuss and agree objectives

Engage people with the task that needs to be completed. Everyone needs to understand your thinking, agree with the plan and be clear about what needs to be done and when. Consider constructive criticisms because it can improve your plan and gain the buy-in of others.

4 Put resources and power in place

Provide the necessary resources and authority. In this way, your people can make decisions and act. Support your people whenever this is needed – they need to know you are behind them.

5 Monitor progress

Ensure that people are accountable for delivering what is expected of them. Having overall goals and interim targets will help people to stay focused, to meet deadlines and to ensure that standards and results are met. The goal is to keep people motivated and on track and to provide additional support where needed.

6 Review progress

Learn from experience and feedback. Compare and discuss results and objectives with those involved. Look at what worked well and what could have been done better. Use this to improve future plans.

KOTTER'S EIGHT-STAGE PROCESS FOR LEADING CHANGE

Achieving progress and getting the right things done in the best way possible

The eight-stage process of creating major change was first outlined by John Kotter in his bestselling book *Leading Change*; it describes what the leader needs to do to ensure that beneficial change is achieved.

1 Establish a sense of urgency

As a leader, you should initiate or take control of the process by emphasizing the need for change. The more urgent and pressing the need, the more likely people will be focused. Usually, the leader's role is to stay positive and build on success. However, it can also help to emphasize failure – what might go wrong and how, when and what the consequences could be. You can also emphasize positive elements such as windows of opportunity that require swift and effective change.

2 Create the guiding coalition

The guiding coalition needs to understand the purpose of the change process. Members should be united, co-ordinated and carry significant authority. The coalition needs to have the power to make things happen, to change systems and procedures, and to win people over.

3 Develop a vision and strategy

The guiding coalition needs to create a simple, powerful vision that will direct and guide change and achieve goals. You need to develop a detailed strategy for achieving that vision. The strategy needs to be practical, workable, understandable, simple and consistent.

4 Communicate the change vision

Use every means possible to constantly communicate the new vision and strategies. This will build pressure, momentum and understanding, sustaining a sense of urgency. The guiding coalition should lead by example and act as role models for the behaviour expected of employees.

5 Empower broad-based action

The leader and the guiding coalition cannot achieve change in isolation – it needs the commitment and effort of others. Provide a blame-free and supportive environment and empower your people by removing obstacles, changing systems or structures that undermine the vision and encouraging risk-taking and non-traditional ideas.

6 Generate short-term wins

These produce momentum and provide an opportunity to build on success. To do this, plan for visible improvements in performance – or 'wins', create those wins and recognize and reward people who make wins possible.

7 Consolidate gains and produce more change

Once the excitement of the start-up phase has passed, the successes have been built and people know what is needed, people can tire and problems can arise. The key is to move steadily: maintain momentum without moving too fast. You need to continue by using increased credibility and understanding of what is still needed, hiring, promoting and developing people who can implement the changes and reinvigorating the process with new projects, themes and change agents.

8 Anchor new approaches in the organization's culture

A key danger in managing change is to finish too early. The best situation is often where change, development and continuous improvements become the norm. What matters is making changes that are firmly grounded in the organization. This requires you to explain the connections between the new behaviours or actions and success.

SIX PRINCIPLES FOR GAINING COMMITMENT

Achieving employee engagement during times of transition

What is the goal of employee engagement? Quite simply: to maximize performance and profit. These will not happen if leaders don't have their people's commitment. Gone are the times when leaders simply informed others; nowadays a dialogue needs to take place. People need to feel valued and listened to, and leaders need to inspire, win hearts and minds, and harness talent and potential.

Successful transitions depend on gaining commitment. Without it, companies underperform and strategy is harder to achieve. John Smythe developed six principles to engage employees – releasing creativity, raising productivity and promoting commitment and loyalty. They give people a compelling reason to work for you, to excel, and to implement plans successfully. By listening, engaging, empowering and encouraging people to share ideas, you will build confidence, loyalty and camaraderie.

1 Develop the right plan and make sure that everyone agrees

Ensure that the senior team has explored all options and developed the best strategy. While teams often agree on a plan, some people may have held back ideas or not been on board. Making sure that everyone at the senior level is on board is critical.

2 Plan the transition process and prepare a timeline

When planning the timeline for implementation, consider the timing of all demands that will be placed on people, including emotional and motivational aspects.

3 Decide who is to be involved – and how

Make sure that everyone is clear about *who* is involved and *how* and *why* they are involved – or affected. When people know what their role is and understand your strategy, they are more engaged, adaptable and committed.

4 Set standards (including role modelling and measuring progress)

Putting standards and timed goals in place enables people to measure progress. The key is to win and maintain people's commitment: measures need to work with people; they should not demotivate. When setting goals, consider the people involved – ask yourself how they would respond.

5 Connect with each person as an individual

Include opportunities for people to reflect, learn and enjoy working for your company. Implementing a new strategy should be enjoyable – emphasize the excitement, the potential and the opportunities. Include opportunities to celebrate past achievements – moving to the future without a nod to the past is discouraging.

6 Tell and sell the new strategy

Tap into people's desire to be part of something and interpret situations from their perspective. Empathy is an invaluable tool for generating enthusiasm and commitment. Remember: the version of change you are giving is not the only one people hear. Be honest, keep people informed, and offer a better, more inspirational and convincing explanation of events and strategy.

BELBIN'S TEAM ROLES

Building, managing and understanding teams and teamworking

R. Meredith Belbin identified nine ways people work together in teams. Understanding these types will help you build and lead better teams.

Leading a team

While people can have characteristics from different categories, one style tends to dominate. To manage teams effectively, you need to identify and understand the style each person uses. Knowing the type of person each team member is will help you to build the right team, get the most out of people, delegate effectively and manage situations successfully. The information can be used to motivate, secure commitment, encourage the behaviours and actions you are looking for, and help you understand when to challenge and when to hold back. This insight enables you to know what type of support to offer, as well as knowing how to avoid conflict or manage it effectively should it arise.

Belbin's nine team roles

Team role	Strengths – contribution to team-working	Weaknesses – problems for team-working
Plant	Plants are creative and imaginative individuals. Their approach can be unorthodox, unusual or freethinking. As a result, they are particularly effective at solving difficult problems.	A propensity to ignore details and become too preoccupied or focused on one issue, hindering communication and collaboration.
Resource investigator	Typically resource investigators are outgoing, extrovert, enthusiastic and communicative. Skills include the ability to explore opportunities and develop contacts.	Over-optimistic and positive, rather than realistic or resilient. This can mean that they lose interest after their initial enthusiasm.
Co-ordinator	Co-ordinators are mature and confident, able to connect big-picture thinking with detailed implementation, good planning and organizational skills.	Too much delegation and co-ordination of others can be seen as manipulative, and they can sometimes be perceived as offloading work.

Team role	Strengths – contribution to team-working	Weaknesses – problems for team-working
Shaper	Shapers are challenging, action-oriented and dynamic. Within teams they enjoy decision-making and problem-solving, and bring the drive and courage needed to overcome obstacles.	Prone to provocation, and may risk offending team-members' feelings with their focus on action and results (rather than people).
Monitor evaluator	Monitor evaluators' strength is their sober, strategic and discerning approach. They contribute to team effectiveness by viewing all options and displaying sound, accurate judgement.	An ability to monitor, evaluate and assess is not always dynamic, and their weaknesses can include a lack of drive and ability to inspire others.
Teamworker	Teamworkers are especially co-operative, perceptive and diplomatic. They complement a team with their ability to listen, build on ideas, promote collaboration and mutual support and avoid friction.	A key weakness is indecision in crunch situations, including those scenarios where there is no 'right' way forward.
Implementer	Implementers contribute to teams by being disciplined, reliable and efficient. They are especially skilled at turning ideas into practical actions and results.	Can slow down teamworking by being inflexible or slow to respond to new options.
Completer finisher	Completer finishers deliver on time and succeed by providing the team with a conscientious, anxious approach that looks for errors and omissions.	Completer finishers can worry unnecessarily or excessively and sometimes be reluctant to delegate.
Specialist	Specialists are single-minded, dedicated self-starters, who contribute to team effectiveness by providing valuable knowledge and skills.	The specialist's weakness is their tendency to concentrate on technicalities and they may only contribute in a single narrow area.

The diagnostic questionnaire for Belbin's team role analysis is available at Belbin Associates' website (www.belbin.com).

DRIVERS OF TRUST AND THE TRUST CYCLE

What we look for when choosing to trust someone

The drivers of trust are the attributes that lead to effective relationships. The cycle of trust is the process through which trust can be developed and maintained.

Overview

Trust matters because success can be achieved only by working through others. By inspiring trust, you will encourage those around you to be flexible and collaborative. Developing the drivers of trust and maintaining the trust of others will lead to productive business relationships.

The drivers of trust

The main drivers of trust are:

- fairness
- dependability
- respect
- openness
- courage

- unselfishness
- competence
- supportiveness
- empathy
- compassion.

By promoting these qualities, relationships with colleagues, customers and stakeholders are more beneficial to everyone involved.

The reality of trust

In reality, the attributes we are more likely to encounter (the reality of trust) are:

- likeability
- dependability
- critical
- ambition
- fairness

- professionalism
- competence
- respect
- controlling
- predictability.

The trust deficit

People look for the drivers of trust when deciding when, and how much, to trust someone. When people's expectations are not met, trust and indeed the entire relationship are seriously undermined. It would seem that without a concerted effort to develop and demonstrate these qualities we are unlikely to develop the rapport we need for good working relationships. Avoiding a trust deficit becomes all-important if we are to get the most out of business relationships. By understanding the drivers of trust, along with the cycle of trust, we can better shape the way we relate to others and build successful, reliable and productive relationships.

The Trust Cycle

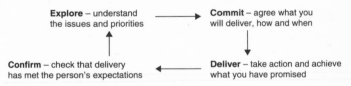

Explore – understand the issues and priorities ⟶ **Commit** – agree what you will deliver, how and when

Confirm – check that delivery has met the person's expectations ⟵ **Deliver** – take action and achieve what you have promised

By continually following these stages, you will build and maintain the trust that is essential for effective, productive relationships. As trust is such a fragile commodity, failing to achieve any one of these stages will damage the relationship and require you to go back and rebuild it. For this reason, ensuring that trust is maintained – by continually developing the drivers of trust and following the cycle of trust – is less disruptive, less time-consuming and less stressful. It creates the positive and productive relationships that are necessary for success.

BUSINESS STRATEGY, PLANNING AND ORGANIZATIONAL EFFECTIVENESS

THE TRUTHS OF STRATEGY

Who, what, how: succeeding with business strategy

Developing a distinctive, successful business strategy is often over-elaborate and over-complicated. Strategy is simply about understanding where you are now, where you are heading and – crucially – how you will get there.

The idea

Strategy has three essential elements: development, implementation and selling (meaning, obtaining commitment and buy-in). Underpinning all three is choice, in particular the need to choose a distinctive strategic position on three dimensions:

1 Who to target as customers (and who to avoid targeting)
2 What products to offer
3 How to undertake related activities efficiently.

In practice

Strategy is all about making tough choices in these three dimensions: who, what and how. It means deciding on the customers you will target and, just as importantly, the customers you will *not* target. This issue requires a focus on customer segmentation and geography.

Delivering a successful strategy also means choosing the products or services you will offer and what product features or benefits to emphasize. Finally, strategy means choosing the activities you will use to sell your selected product to your selected customer.

This approach sounds simple but there are several key points to note to ensure a successful strategy:

- **Ensure that your strategy creates a unique strategic position.** This is achieved by focusing on who your customers are, the value proposition offered to these customers and how you can do this efficiently.
- **Make distinctive, tough choices.** To be distinctive and meaningful, strategy must make difficult choices and combine these choices in a self-reinforcing system of activities that fit. Common mistakes include: keeping options open; permitting incentives in the system that enable people to ignore choices; searching for growth in a way that forces people to ignore the firm's strategy, and analysis paralysis.
- **Understand the importance of values and incentives.** In particular, the underlying environment of your organization creates the behaviours of that organization. The organization's culture and values, measurement and incentives, people, structure and processes all determine the underlying environment.
- **Gain people's emotional commitment to the strategy.** Any strategy, however brilliant, will fail unless people are emotionally committed to its success.
- **Remember, understanding is not the same as communicating.** Explain why the strategy is important to the organization and the individual.
- **Do not overlook the knowledge–doing gap.** Individuals tend to do the urgent things and not the important ones. There is a gap between what they know and what they do. Remember, what gets measured gets done.
- **Do not believe that 'strategic' means important.** Closely linked is the mistaken view that only 'top' people can develop strategic ideas. Ideas can come from anybody, any time, anywhere.
- **Keep your strategy flexible.** All ideas are good for a limited time – not for ever. Keep checking the answers to the 'who – what – how' questions. Strategy does not need to be changed too often but it will occasionally require adjusting to suit external circumstances. So, give your people freedom and autonomy to respond and to adjust, without waiting for permission or instructions.

SWOT ANALYSIS

A valuable decision-making technique

SWOT analysis can work at many different levels: from the overall operation of the organization as a whole to the separate and independent issues affecting a department or a single product.

- Strengths
- Opportunities
- Weaknesses
- Threats

Internal sources of strength and weakness

These are typically found within an organization, whereas opportunities and threats are most often external. Some factors can be sources both of strength and weakness: for example the age of employees. Older employees may denote a stable organization, able to retain employees and maintain a wealth of experience, or it may simply mean that the organization is too conservative. Many factors can be either strengths or weaknesses and they can change from one to the other surprisingly quickly.

External sources of opportunity and threat

These are more difficult to assess than internal ones. Examples of sources of opportunities and threats are detailed below.

Sources of opportunity include:

- new markets (including export markets)
- new technologies
- new products and product enhancements
- mergers, acquisitions and divestments
- new investment
- factors affecting competitors' fortunes
- commercial agreements and strategic partnerships
- political, economic, regulatory and trade developments.

Sources of threats include:

- industrial action
- political and regulatory issues
- economic issues
- trade factors
- mergers and other developments among competitors
- new market entrants
- pricing actions by competitors
- market innovations by competitors
- environmental factors
- natural disasters
- crises, notably including issues of health, safety, product quality and liability
- key staff attracted away from the business
- security issues, including industrial espionage and the security of IT systems
- supply chain problems
- distribution and delivery problems
- bad debts (resulting from the fortunes of others)
- demographic factors and social changes affecting customers' tastes or habits.

SCENARIO THINKING

Walking the battlefield before battle commences

Scenario thinking is a tool for exploring possible futures. It is used to stimulate debate, develop resilient strategies and test business plans against possible futures. It enables us to think innovatively and to develop strategy that is not constrained by the past. It provides the insight needed to manage uncertainty and risk, set strategy, handle complexity, improve decision-making, reveal current potential, promote responsiveness and control our future.

Overview

Scenarios inform and guide our understanding of possible futures that lie ahead and the forces contributing to those events. The outcomes of different responses to potential developments can be tested, without risk, through exploring various scenarios. The aim is not to predict the future accurately but to experience events before they happen.

Scenario thinking allows us to:

- reveal new perspectives and identify gaps in organizational knowledge
- challenge assumptions, overcoming business-as-usual thinking
- understand the present and identify potential
- promote awareness of external events
- encourage people to share information and ideas
- improve our responses to events
- promote a shift in attitude and develop greater certainty
- promote a shared purpose and direction.

The Strategic Conversation is an ongoing process of assessing the present, creating and testing scenarios, developing and analysing options, and then selecting, refining and implementing the chosen options. Scenarios should:

- involve people at all levels
- be relevant and valued
- avoid existing biases
- be rooted in a thorough analysis of the present.

Initial planning

Create a separate team to plan the process – preferably external people known for innovative, challenging thinking. They should:

- identify gaps in knowledge, given the business challenges to be faced
- agree the project's duration
- interview members of the scenario workshop – asking each person for a 'history of the future' (what could happen and how it happened)
- collate and analyse their responses in a report, identifying the main issues, ideas and uncertainties. (This will set the agenda for the first workshop.)

Developing the scenarios

The aim is to understand the forces shaping the future. The workshop should develop scenarios that create and assess possible events and their consequences. Participants should:

- identify the forces that could impact a situation
- agree two possible opposite outcomes (and the forces involved)
- identify how these forces are linked
- decide whether each force has a low or high impact and a low or high probability
- develop likely 'histories' that led to each outcome, detailing the factors involved.

Analysing and using the scenarios

Identify the priorities and concerns of people responsible for key decisions in the scenario who are outside the organization – including their likely reactions at different stages in the scenario. Then develop an action plan by working backwards from the scenario's future to the present in order to identify the early signs of change. These can be recognized and acted upon swiftly and effectively, thereby influencing the strategic direction of the company.

THE BALANCED SCORECARD

Developed by Robert Kaplan and David Norton, the Balanced Scorecard is a valuable adjunct to traditional business measures that are limited by their focus on past performance. The Balanced Scorecard overcomes this limitation by providing a means of assessing future performance to better inform and guide strategic development.

Overview

The reason for its success is its ability to integrate measures of performance to present a balanced view of a company's overall performance and to pinpoint areas that need completion or further development. The process generates objectives in four areas – financial data, customers' perceptions, essential internal processes, and innovation and learning – and puts in place action plans and continuous assessment. It has been criticized for being too prescriptive and quantitative, but its use can be broadened to include qualitative aspects.

How to use the Balanced Scorecard approach

The approach taken will depend on the company's type, size and structure. However, there are five broad stages:

1 **Prepare, define and communicate the strategy** – people need to understand the objectives and how to achieve them.
2 **Decide what to measure** – typical measures are shown in this table:

Area	Aim	What to measure
Financial	To increase: • profitability • share price performance • return on assets	• Cash flows • Cost reduction • Gross margins • Return on capital / equity / investments / sales • Revenue growth • Payment terms

Area	Aim	What to measure
Customers	To improve: • customer acquisition • customer retention • customer satisfaction • cross-sales volumes	• Market share • Customer service and satisfaction • Number of complaints • Customer profitability • Delivery times • Units sold • Number of customers
Internal processes	To improve: • core competencies • critical technologies • employee morale … and to: • streamline processes	• Efficiency • Lead times • Unit costs • Waste • Sourcing and supplier delivery • Employee morale and satisfaction, and staff turnover • Internal audit standards • Sales per employee
Innovation and learning	To promote: • new product development • continuous improvement • employees' training and skills	• Number of new products • Sales of new products • Number of employees receiving training • Outputs from employees' training • Training hours per employee • Number and scope of skills learned

3 **Finalize and implement the plan** – this stage ensures that measures are workable, tailored and adopted. Essentially, this is managing by setting objectives.

4 **Publicize and use the results** – being seen to act is important. Also, while ensuring that everyone understands overall objectives, decide who should receive specific information, why and how frequently.

5 **Review and amend the system** – to solve any problems and to set new challenges.

THE 7S MODEL

Assessing business performance

The 7S model is a framework for assessing the performance of a company. It views all seven elements as equally important because they impact on each other – with failure in one area undermining the others. By appreciating how they are related, and assessing performance from this perspective, companies and teams can better align activities to achieve goals.

Overview

First developed in the 1970s by McKinsey and refined by Tom Peters, Robert Waterman and Richard Pascale, the 7S model works from the principle that success relies on simultaneously pursuing a combination of seven hard and soft aspects of running a business. Known for changing people's thinking at the time, it still provides a useful framework for assessing and improving a company or how a team is working – identifying gaps and enabling adjustments to be made to ensure that all seven aspects are aligned, working together, and supporting and reinforcing one another. By knowing how things are interrelated, the framework raises awareness of the full impact of any changes.

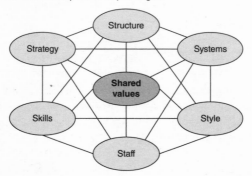

1 Strategy

These are plans that determine, define and outline how to fulfil the company's goals and purpose and to achieve competitive advantage.

2 Structure

This is how the company is organized and how each part relates to the others.

3 Systems

This is about how both formal and informal business processes function.

4 Shared values (superordinate goals)

These are the company's beliefs, values and guiding mission that draw people together and that directly influence their approach, thinking and actions.

5 Skills

These are the capabilities of both the people and the organization.

6 Staff

This concerns the nature, type and general abilities of the people employed.

7 Style

This is the organization's culture and style of leadership that, along with having an internal impact, determine how people outside the organization view the company.

The main point is that all seven elements are interrelated, with each affecting the others. In this, it can be viewed as an early proponent of holistic business. Significantly – and this is of particular relevance to leaders today – it reveals how underperformance can be attributed to neglect in any one of the seven aspects, regardless of strong focus and capabilities in one or more of the others. Richard Pascale subsequently argued that, while it is generally important to view all seven as equally significant to achieving success, having shared values (superordinate goals) is the element that binds all the others together.

THE RULE OF 150

A bold way to create the right working conditions

This rule is about limiting the number of people at any one location to 150.

Overview

The rule is based on the idea that 150 is the largest group size that people can deal with – beyond that number, it is increasingly difficult to form bonds with others. If groups are larger, hierarchies, regulations and formal measures are required. However, with fewer than 150, goals can be achieved informally and people work better and are happier, more motivated and more productive.

Why it works

Co-workers find socializing, teamworking, innovating, collaborating and sharing knowledge easier to achieve in groups of fewer than 150 people. By organizing operations into smaller groups, large companies can gain the benefit of smaller groups – being closer, driven, entrepreneurial, supportive and productive.

The rule in practice

Gore Associates, a high-tech firm, uses this rule. It has 15 plants all within 20 kilometres (12 miles) of one another, and each with fewer than 150 employees. It has resisted the option of merging its separate sites – despite potential cost savings – because the small size of each unit ensures that everyone knows everyone else and works well together.

By organizing itself in this way, Gore, despite being a large company with thousands of employees, is still able to enjoy the entrepreneurial approach of a small start-up. Each unit enjoys the benefits of collective management, which are:

- improved communication
- greater initiative
- flexibility.

It is notable that employee turnover is significantly less than the industry average and the company has enjoyed sustained profitability and growth for over 35 years.

This does not mean that Gore has no control or input. It has put a strong managerial system in place to oversee each unit, to ensure that activities are co-ordinated and efficient. The company also encourages a sense of community and teamwork within these groups – after all, the rule only means that it is *possible* for workers to form positive bonds with each other, so efforts must still be made to ensure that this happens. In addition, Gore makes sure that it develops a sense of community across the company by encouraging people to communicate and collaborate with workers from other groups.

THE SERVICE PROFIT CHAIN

Managing the vital link between people and profit

The service profit chain highlights how employee engagement drives improvements in company performance. When employees are able to see the impact of their actions, it changes their approach and improves results.

The idea

The service profit chain is based on the premise that market leadership requires an emphasis on managing value drivers – those factors that have the greatest impact on success and provide the most benefit to customers. This concept is then focused on the value drivers that are the most important determinants of success: employee retention, employee satisfaction and employee productivity – it is these that strongly influence customer loyalty, revenue growth and profitability.

How the service profit chain works

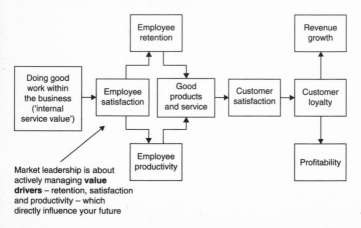

Market leadership is about actively managing **value drivers** – retention, satisfaction and productivity – which directly influence your future

In practice: Sears

In the 1990s US-based retailer Sears reversed significant losses by focusing on employee issues in order to turn around the company's fortunes. They examined:

- how employees felt about working at the company
- how employee behaviour affected customers
- how customers' experience affected profits.

Sears asked employees to estimate how much profit was made for each dollar sold. The average answer was 46 cents while the real answer was *1 cent* – demonstrating that profitability was poorly understood. The company introduced changes in order to engage with employees and to get them to understand what influences profitability – in particular, to make clear the link between employee behaviour, customer satisfaction and company success. By understanding the implications of their actions, it changed their approach, resulting in sustained improvements in profitability.

In practice: B&Q

At UK retailer B&Q, each percentage increase in staff turnover was costing the company £1 million. By reducing staff turnover from 35 to 28 per cent through its Employee Engagement Programme, the company reduced costs and increased turnover per employee by 20 per cent.

UNDERSTANDING AND AVOIDING ACTIVE INERTIA

When success traps us in the past

It might seem counterintuitive to warn people about the dangers of success but that is exactly what Donald Sull did when he developed the concept of 'active inertia' – where people repeat the strategies and activities that have worked well in the past.

A reliance on previous thinking and approaches – the formula of success – can cause a company to fail to respond properly to new developments. By applying past approaches to new conditions, the end result can be a downward spiral – leaving an organization vulnerable to more dynamic companies with approaches better suited to the new environment.

How active inertia works

A firm correctly discerns gradual shifts and developments in the external environment, but fails to respond effectively.

↓

Managers get trapped by success, often responding to the most disruptive changes by accelerating activities that succeeded in the past.

↓

The source of active inertia is a company's success formula, the unique set of strategic frames, resources, processes, relationships and values that collectively influence managers' actions.

↓

With time and repetition, people stop considering alternatives to their formula. The individual components of the success formula grow less flexible.

How active inertia happens

Active inertia occurs because people come to rely on a past formula of success, where accepted approaches become entrenched and people stop considering alternatives. Consequently, people continue to respond to external changes by pursuing fixes and activities that worked in the past. However, these responses are likely to be ineffectual because they are based on past success and not current and future needs.

Why a past success formula does not guarantee a successful future

Essentially, like it or not, our brains are lazy – subconsciously preferring the easy route to solving problems and then, equally subconsciously, superimposing a solid layer of reasons to justify our decisions. So it is hardly surprising that our brains fool us into being happy to rely on approaches that have proven successful in the past: it is easy and we have a ready-made wall of rock-solid excuses to hand.

As individuals, our thinking, strategies, methods, use of resources, relationships and values all become firmly entrenched. The consequence for companies is that this formula becomes so deeply embedded that they are left vulnerable when faced with changing conditions.

It is understandable that past approaches should be so revered and relied upon – they are, after all, the reason for the company's current success. However, we should keep in mind that this formula is exactly that: suited to the current, stable situation – not the future. Companies can suddenly find themselves commercially stranded.

The bottom line is that, when faced with new developments, your approach needs to change accordingly – essentially, the survival of the fittest depends on adaptation.

THE SIX Rs OF BUSINESS

Business is a total activity

Luis Gallardo's Six Rs is a total approach to business – where all activities work together, moving the whole company forward in the same direction.

Having all company activities support one other enables us to develop the right mindset, strategy and approach for growing a successful business. This holistic approach ensures that no part of a company undermines overall goals or the activities of another part of the business. The Six Rs are:

- Reason
- Revenue
- Rousers

- Reputation
- Relationships
- Resilience.

Why the Six Rs matter

The Six Rs should work together, supporting one other and never undermining other business activities or goals. As companies can discover to their cost (witness the damage to sales when legal tax avoidance is revealed), any aspect of running a business can have serious consequences. Conversely, when the various corporate activities support one other, they will strengthen the brand and promote success. Essentially, everyone and all activities should pull together. To have parts, even unwittingly, pulling in different directions will derail strategy and cause a company to veer off course.

Reason

The starting point, and ongoing requirement, for setting and directing all activities is to know the reason why you are in business – your vision, values and purpose. This sets the tone and gains commitment and, consequently, has an enormous impact on customers and achieving goals. Your purpose should be communicated to everyone in the organization. Also, by fitting your products and services to your reason and values, customers and employees will understand what your company means.

Revenue

Managing and maximizing revenues is essential for enacting strategies and building resilience. An often overlooked but critical aspect is the portfolio of clients – it reveals strengths and gaps elsewhere in the company. The important thing is to manage revenues through the prism of the rest of the 6Rs – and to manage the others through the lens of revenue.

Rousers

Engaging your people and aligning their thinking and behaviours to the rest of the company's activities depend on being able to inspire them. This has an enormous impact on all areas of a business – especially customers – and sets the right conditions for people to be innovative and to adapt successfully to change.

Reputation

Reputation is critical to success. It affects employees as well as current and potential customers and all stakeholders. The important point is that reputation can be affected by any aspect of the business – emphasizing the need to ensure that other activities do not undermine reputation.

Relationships

All business – internal and external – is about handling relationships. Everything is affected, with a direct bearing on profitability, so all relationships should be managed carefully, keeping in mind the importance of the Six Rs approach.

Resilience

Developing resilience enables companies to continue achieving goals, to survive difficult circumstances and to take advantage of opportunities. It enables swift and appropriate responses to any developments and the flexibility to adapt to change. Resilience involves being proactive, prepared and having the right mindset to deal with any events, threats or opportunities.

THE BOSTON CONSULTING GROUP MODEL

How to manage your product portfolio

Identifying which products and investments should be continued (and at what level of investment) is a complicated task. Cutting through this confusion, the Boston Consulting Group model (developed by Bruce Henderson) provides a straightforward means of managing your portfolio of products.

How it works

The model uses a matrix, each box representing a type of product: Star, Cash cow, Question mark and Dog. Products are located in a quadrant according to market growth and market share. The category a product falls into enables you to see whether it is worth pursuing. By looking at the matrix, it is easy to see why each category has certain characteristics and prospects.

Star

Given the high market growth, this product is obviously a rising star and should be pursued. Coupled with high market share, the risks are minimal and the return will be high. A note of caution, though, is that a growing market will inevitably cost a lot to keep up with so it is advisable to consider your ability to fund this – especially if there are large set-up costs or if you expect a delay in the product generating revenue.

Cash cow

Clearly, given the large market share, there is still a lot of potential for generating revenue. However, given the low market growth, there may be some limiting factors (such as time or changing technology) that suggest you should milk these products as much as you can before the opportunity for high returns dwindles in a declining market. It would be wise to monitor market conditions closely to prevent losses should the market decline rapidly.

Question mark

If a product falls into this category, there are issues that need to be addressed before a decision can be made. Although there is high market growth, you have to ask yourself whether the low market share will generate enough revenue to justify the investment – especially given the likely high costs of keeping pace with a growing market. A key factor in making a decision is having deep-enough pockets either to wait for higher returns as the market grows or to turn it into a Star by securing a stronger market share.

Dog

With low market share and low market growth, this product is going nowhere fast. Clearly, it is not worth pursuing. Sometimes, you may wish to continue with this type of product if it provides other benefits – such as maintaining customer loyalty for your overall brand.

THE PARETO PRINCIPLE

Finding the right focus and answer using the 80:20 rule

Pareto analysis arose from Vilfredo Pareto's observation that many activities break down into an 80:20 ratio, where 80 per cent of output is due to 20 per cent of the contributory factors. This observation is now used to focus business strategy, problem-solving and operations on the key inputs that are responsible for 80 per cent of the outcome.

How it works

The 80:20 ratio applies both to positive and negative situations, providing a useful means of dealing quickly with problems or opportunities. In other words, by identifying the small number of key factors that are contributing most to a situation, we can better focus efforts to achieve the desired result.

Pareto analysis is only as good as the data that is used, so we need to ensure that all contributory factors are identified and that appropriate and revealing parameters and measures are established and interpreted correctly. Although not everything falls neatly into an 80:20 rule, Pareto analysis is still useful for identifying the main causal factors.

This simple example shows how the process works.

1 Research and discuss the issue, identifying all contributory factors.
2 Decide an appropriate time period and method of measurement.
3 Measure how frequently each factor occurs (or another measure, such as cost).
4 Rank the factors in descending order, with the largest one first.
5 Calculate the frequency of each factor as a percentage of the total occurrences (or cost).

6 Calculate the cumulative percentage (current percentage plus all previous percentages).

7 Depict this information on a graph – with 'frequency as a percentage of total' as a bar chart and 'cumulative percentage' as a line, adding a third line showing the 80 per cent cut-off point.

All factors that appear to the left of the intersection of the two lines are the ones contributing to 80 per cent of the result – these are the factors to focus on.

Example of how the Pareto Principle can be displayed

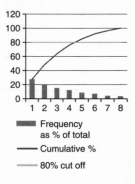

Frequency
as % of total

Cumulative %

80% cut off

Factor	Frequency	Frequency as % of total	Cumulative %
1	570	27.6	27.6
2	425	20.6	48.2
3	320	15.5	63.9
4	255	12.4	76.0
5	180	8.7	84.8
6	150	7.3	92.0
7	90	4.4	96.4
8	75	3.6	100

BLUE OCEAN STRATEGY

Creating unique market opportunities

A Blue Ocean Strategy is one where the key to success lies not in competing directly with rivals within a market, but in *creating an entirely new market* where there are currently no competitors and where the potential for high returns is vast.

Developed by W. Chan Kim and Renée Mauborgne, Blue Ocean Strategy involves a change in strategic thinking towards a mindset that challenges existing market boundaries, rewrites the rules of competition, and creates a new, as yet uncontested, market space. The theory outlines two attitudes to competition: Red Oceans and Blue Oceans.

The current marketplace for all products and services is made up of **Red Oceans** (bloody battlegrounds), where boundaries are clearly defined and companies operate within the boundaries of their accepted Red Ocean markets. Here, the entrenched battleground is one where companies compete to gain extra market share within the current market boundary.

A very different attitude pervades the **Blue Oceans**. These are areas of deep, uncharted, almost limitless potential where the aim is not to compete on traditional grounds but to develop products and services that create entirely new markets. In essence, it is creating customers that do not yet exist.

At its core, Blue Ocean Strategy believes that it is better to create tomorrow's customers through developing a new market rather than scrabbling around trying to capture existing customers in the current marketplace. There may be many justifications for this approach but, quite simply, the reason seems straightforward: to create a monopoly situation and reap the high rewards before competitors enter the new market.

Value creation

Value is achieved by integrating the utility of the product with its cost and price. It is not a case of choosing between competing through managing costs or product differentiation: it is about pursuing both. It is this that creates the value that appeals across customer groups, drawing them into a new market. Think of this as maximizing the gap between the utility of the product and its price (facilitated by lower costs) – the larger this gap, the higher the value and the more it attracts customers.

Blue Ocean Strategy relies on four main principles:

1 **Challenging existing market boundaries.** Reconstruct the marketplace, identifying and creating new markets and customers. The Blue Ocean is a vast place where demand is unrealized – it doesn't yet exist. The aim is to bring this demand into existence.
2 **Keeping focused on the overall picture.** Be clear about your goals: what matters and needs to be achieved.
3 **Minimizing risk.** Assess current industry standards and decide what can be:
   a   eliminated – things that are not necessary
   b   reduced – things that do not need to be done to a high standard
   c   raised – things that should be done better
   d   created – things that have never been offered before.
4 **Planning careful implementation.** You will need to overcome barriers and secure the resources and the support of your people (especially key influencers).

BENCHMARKING

Measuring performance

Benchmarking establishes standards against which performance can be measured. It is used to assess performance and to set targets across a range of business activities.

Overview

The purpose of benchmarking is to improve efficiency and quality, to determine and promote best practice, to maintain competitiveness and to focus people on the need for change and improvement. Carol McNair and Kathleen Leibfried divide benchmarking into four categories as shown in this table:

Category	Aim
Internal	Using internal measures to match or surpass current performance, ensure consistent standards throughout the company, eliminate waste and improve operations
Competitive	Using competitors' standards to set targets that match or improve upon their performance
Industry	Setting benchmarks that are industry standards
Best	To match or surpass the standards of the best companies in any industry or country

Setting benchmarks

The data should be free from bias or vested interests. Using an external company to gather evidence and measure standards will help to maintain impartiality.

Successful benchmarking needs everyone to be 'on the same page' and to understand the process. People need to be clear about what is being measured and why, and it is important to give people the time and resources they need.

While targets need to be realistic and achievable, they also need to ensure that standards are maintained and consistent throughout a company and they should seek to continually improve upon performance. To do this, it is necessary to look at both internal and external evidence.

Benchmarking is a continual process that needs to adapt quickly to changes – it is no use measuring activities that are no longer relevant or failing to measure activities that are now more significant. To do this effectively, as well as assessing internal operations, you need a keen awareness of your customers, competitors and companies in other sectors. This ensures that benchmarking is focused on the issues that matter now rather than reflecting the past, and is not blinkered by a narrow, internal focus that risks delivering more of the same.

By enabling you to know what competitors are doing and what the most innovative, high-performing companies in other industries are achieving, benchmarking will help to maintain your company's competitiveness.

THE PRODUCT LIFE CYCLE

Managing your product portfolio

From development and launch, through its peak to eventual decline, a product's life cycle determines the strategy needed to optimize its return at each stage and to develop further products to ensure ongoing profitability and competitiveness.

Although not an exact science, the duration of each stage varies according to the product and the markets involved. Some life cycles are obviously shorter than others – such as technology products. With very short life cycles, it is essential to maximize returns as quickly as possible and to be continually developing the next products. A long-lasting branded product, despite undergoing many life cycles, enjoys continuity from its brand name. Companies, however, still have to manage the life cycles of such branded products – planning the next improvement and managing the replacement of the current version.

There are five stages in the product life cycle:

1 **Development** – this includes entirely new products and changes or improvements to existing products
2 **Introduction** – at this stage, costs can be high relative to revenue
3 **Growth** – revenue rises and offsets costs
4 **Maturity** – growth slows and competition rises
5 **Decline** – sales decline due to increased competition or changing customer preferences

The following describes tactics appropriate to each stage:

Development

Development can be very costly, with unexpected delays, so cash-flow issues are paramount. Researching what customers are looking for and testing prototypes with potential customers will help you develop the right products with fewer glitches – as well as promoting a ready-made pool of customers. Importantly, product development is an ongoing process, ensuring that new products or improvements to existing products are ready to replace current products.

chapter 29

Introduction

Getting the launch right is essential. Raising product awareness quickly requires promotional and advertising investment – depending on the nature of the product, targeting early adopters can be useful at this stage. An aggressive pricing strategy can achieve fast market penetration – although this will depend on the brand's attributes. You could also consider minimizing distribution costs by limiting the availability of the product.

Growth

In the face of more competition, but still with considerable potential revenue and falling unit costs, strategy needs to focus on outcompeting rivals, delivering extra value to customers and increasing market share. Further promotional offers, marketing and advertising campaigns, attractive prices and promoting the product's brand will strengthen your position.

Maturity

Given the influx of competitors, a company is faced with several strategic options to strengthen its market share, including: product differentiation, entering new markets, attracting rivals' customers, a price war, and reducing costs to maintain competitive pricing and profitability. It is important at this stage to monitor the financial situation and the viability of the different options.

Decline

With falling sales and reduced margins, any plans and further investment should be considered carefully. Reducing the available options for the product and reducing the number of markets the product is offered in will reduce costs. Catering to your core customers to cement their loyalty can also boost profits at this stage. Other tactics to extend the life of a product include product extensions and entering previously untapped markets.

SYSTEMS THINKING

Building better companies

A company is a collection of systems, and systems within systems. These all need to operate individually and collectively, to drive the business forward. A company's systems need to work with strategy, and they need to be open, adaptive and understood.

Traditional approaches to strategy have emphasized the mechanics of how things work. This can result in too much complexity and 'over-engineering', with processes and systems being overly focused on the present, unable to adapt and failing to win people over. The fundamental flaw is setting a predetermined solution at the start of any redesign, which then influences subsequent thinking, narrowing views and ambitions, and misses better options. Often, the result of re-engineering is an expensive disappointment.

In *The Fifth Discipline*, Peter Senge revolutionized business re-engineering by arguing that solutions should be considered only after fully understanding the relationships within and between systems (including the behaviours involved) and examining all related problems and issues. Essentially: go back to basics, look deeper and search further, before you start thinking about solutions. Such open systems thinking builds teams, promotes creativity and develops new approaches. It works with the company's long-term strategy, enabling adaptability and continual improvement. It is not the easiest approach: it is time-consuming and mentally demanding and generates an overwhelming number of questions. It works best when the right culture and mindset exist.

There are seven steps to successful systems thinking:

1 Explore the situation

Gather the information you need without making judgements or looking for causes and effects. At this stage, do two things:

- Cast your net wide, collating as much information as possible.
- Be objective and detached (see things as they are, without an agenda).

2 Describe the system

To understand what you are dealing with, list and describe the things that have happened – including the culture, people and atmosphere. Identify, date and examine trends and patterns. Position each factor on a diagram to show the relationships that exist between them. This highlights how aspects work together and reveals negative and positive feedback loops to enable you to analyse the systems in more depth later.

3 Build models

Mathematical and IT tools are useful but they will take you only so far because systems need to be considered as they really function if they are to be understood and improved.

4 Compare your model to what is actually happening

Check your model against reality to see whether it fits and whether you have understood it correctly or have missed something.

5 Identify potential improvements

Once you have confirmed that your model is an accurate representation of what is happening, explore ways in which the system can be improved.

6 Implement your improvements

Monitor changes and identify any further improvements that could be made. It is essential to win people over – successful change depends on people's willingness to work positively with the new systems.

7 Repeat the process

Systems thinking is a continuous activity; companies need to adapt to change and to take advantage of new opportunities.

MARKET BARRIERS

Protecting your profits

Market exit and entry barriers have both positive and negative effects on profit, depending on your company's position and on the impact the barriers have on your competitors. A key aspect of awareness of market barriers is that they increase our focus on external issues. In short, it forces us to look up and see the business horizon in much greater detail.

Overview

The word 'barrier' is slightly misleading. While barriers will certainly make you do your sums, consider the ramifications and prepare contingency plans, they also deter your competitors. And that is the point: use barriers to your advantage. Your strategy must include careful calculations about the costs involved and you must balance these against the revenue and market dominance potential, but it should also look for how to exploit barriers to your advantage.

The matrix below summarizes the impact of barriers to entry and exit on profitability.

	Low exit barriers	High exit barriers
Low entry barriers	Returns: stable Profit: low	Returns: at risk Profit: low
High entry barriers	Returns: stable Profit: high	Returns: at risk Profit: high

Entry barriers

There are many barriers to entry, including:

- the high cost of capital
- other companies owning patents and proprietary technology

- high research and development costs of developing necessary products
- expensive technology
- existing companies enjoying economies of scale that you can't afford to match
- a restricted number of government licences
- the expense of (or lack of access to) effective distribution channels
- your product not being different enough from market leaders.

Exit barriers

There are many exit barriers, including:

- high fixed costs
- few buyers for your expensive, specialized equipment
- contractual salary, redundancy and pension commitments
- legal regulations
- outstanding contractual obligations
- being tied to other companies
- risk to brand image.

Not only do you need to understand all the costs, legalities and brand issues, you need to understand how barriers work: how they affect you and, importantly, how they will affect your current and potential competitors. Do this and you will determine the business strategy that is right for your company.

For example, the ideal scenario for an established company is to have high entry barriers and low exit barriers. The reasons are self-evident: high entry barriers deter others from entering the market you are already operating in; low exit barriers will not cause you a problem should you decide to change course.

A much less favourable scenario is having low entry barriers but high exit barriers. Obviously, with low entry barriers, competitors can flood into the market. Unfortunately, the high exit barriers will make it difficult and expensive to leave the market, restricting your strategic options in the future.

THE SIX Ps OF STRATEGIC THINKING

Following the right path

Strategy is an overused word, but it simply means moving from where you are now to where you want to be. The Six Ps framework helps to guide thinking when developing, implementing, monitoring and reviewing strategy.

Overview

Business strategy is a total activity, with every part of the organization connected and working together successfully. Because of this, some of the best-laid plans can go awry or fail to achieve their potential because of simple oversights or by a failure to properly explore an issue. The Six Ps highlight how all aspects of a business must work together, and how shortcomings in one part will affect other aspects of your strategy.

Using the Six Ps framework will help to keep the strategy focused on the most important issues as well as enabling you to understand exactly what is happening, to look at issues creatively, to develop solutions, to monitor progress and to think strategically.

The Six Ps of stategic thinking are Plan, Ploy, Pattern, Position, Perspective and Process, explained in the following flow chart.

PLAN – Know where you are headed, and design the plan that will get you there.

↓

PLOY – Determine the tactics that will deal effectively with competitors or others in your own company.

↓

PATTERN – Assess the patterns of behaviour that are apparent in order, for example, to improve processes or to identify potential customers and markets.

↓

POSITION – Know where your company fits in the market relative to the competition.

↓

PERSPECTIVE – Assess the current character of the company and consider how this could be improved to better match strategic aims.

↓

PROCESS (programme of activities) – Develop, monitor and improve a programme of activities to achieve your strategy.

PORTER'S GENERIC COMPETITIVE STRATEGIES

Choosing the road ahead

Porter's Generic Competitive Strategies describe how a company develops competitive advantage across its chosen market. There are three generic strategies: cost leadership, differentiation and focus.

Overview

A company chooses to pursue one of two types of *competitive advantage*: either with lower costs than its competitors, or by differentiating itself along dimensions valued by customers so it can command a higher price. A company also chooses one of two types of *scope*: either focus (offering its products to selected segments of the market) or industry-wide, offering its product across many market segments. The generic strategy reflects choices made about both the type of competitive advantage and the scope. The concept was first described by Michael Porter in 1980.

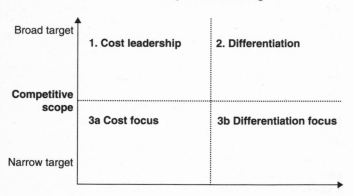

Competitive advantage

	1. Cost leadership	2. Differentiation
Broad target		
Competitive scope		
Narrow target	3a Cost focus	3b Differentiation focus

Cost leadership

The strategic aim is to offer competitive prices by reducing costs and to also use lower costs to raise profit margins, fund discount campaigns, or launch an aggressive price war to gain market share and eliminate the competition. Reducing costs can also open up new markets that were less able to sustain higher prices. Another advantage of lowering costs is providing flexibility should suppliers raise prices unexpectedly and suddenly, without you also having to raise prices.

The risks, however, are that other companies can copy your methods, eroding any advantage you have, and the lack of investment in research and development will leave your products looking dated and inefficient compared to those of competitors with better equipment and methods.

Differentiation

Developing distinctive products for different segments separates you from the competition. It creates product desirability, strengthens your brand, promotes customer loyalty, provides competitive advantage, enables higher prices and delivers higher returns. Your products can be differentiated from those of your competitors but you can also differentiate your own products from one another to target different customer groups and markets.

The risks are higher costs and waste and the potential for more complex operations.

Focus

While focus incorporates aspects of cost leadership and differentiation, it is concerned with targeting products and services at one market segment, gaining increased share in that segment. The risk is that this will produce a narrow view that is overly focused on the short term, on too few factors, and on a less lucrative or unstable market and thus fails to see potential elsewhere.

PESTLIED ANALYSIS

Looking outwards for opportunities

Using PESTLIED analysis improves awareness of the impact of external factors. Given the huge number of influences – both opportunities and threats – it is essential to constantly scan the environment for changes and adjust strategy and operations accordingly.

Overview

When running a business it is always advisable to keep a wide range of external matters in view. PESTLIED provides a format to check that strategy and plans have adequately accounted for external factors and to conduct an overall review of how the company is performing and how it could be improved. Significantly, by valuing and using this format, it encourages people to always look beyond the company to notice opportunities and threats. It therefore works well with the technique of SWOT analysis.

The broad areas to consider that form part of PESTLIED analysis are outlined below.

Political

Consider the governmental actions that could affect your company – from local councils and national governments to larger, supranational bodies.

Economic

Understand all current and potential financial aspects (in different countries) that are either detrimental or offer opportunities – such as taxation, financial regulations, interest rates and currency markets.

Social

Knowing about developing trends, the general mood of a country, and people's beliefs, changes in tastes and fashions and their expectations has always been important, but never more so than today, with the rise and power of social media.

Technical

We are living in an age where knowledge and use of the latest technologies are everything. These can reduce costs and enable us to offer better products and services. It is an inescapable fact: the company that doesn't move with new technology rapidly becomes outdated and out-competed.

Legal

Not conducting due diligence and not knowing exactly what legalities and regulations are involved is irresponsible and risky. While this should be normal in terms of your current places of operation, you should also look to possible future developments and to what is happening (and likely to happen) in other countries. Are there better places to base your operations and will future changes make somewhere else advantageous? When entering new markets, it is important to know all legal aspects so that you set the right strategy and ensure that all legal obligations are met.

International

This is a broad area covering everything from what is happening in international politics and economics to exchange rates and stock markets. The point is: cast your net wide and be aware of changes on the international stage.

Environmental

Your brand is affected by everything your company does, including its environmental policy. You also need to consider current and likely environmental regulations when setting and implementing strategy.

Demographic

Demographic changes have a huge impact on companies and yet they are often poorly understood. This is a serious oversight. Demographics should inform business decisions: not only will it affect the availability of workers and pension obligations, but it will also determine current and future market opportunities.

THE DYNAMICS OF PARADIGM CHANGE

Creating better futures

Introducing changes in an organization is difficult. Changing your entire business model is even harder – not least because the need for such a fundamental shift often doesn't occur to us or is full of the fear of uncertainty. Even so, competition doesn't stand still and companies need to adapt; sometimes the answer may require a shift in the basic paradigm.

Overview

When things need to change, people often prefer manageable adjustments because they are cautious and dislike uncertainty. While some issues can be solved with smaller improvements, sometimes a larger shift in thinking is needed. Having the courage and creativity to change a company's fundamental business model radically isn't easy but may be the only real answer to a problem or even point the way to a better future. After all, your current situation is ultimately resting on the paradigm that has got you to this point. So, tweaking this and that further up the line may help to a degree but may not be tackling the root cause of the problem: a flawed or outdated business model. You are not likely to make significant changes to your situation without questioning the basic paradigm of your company and considering whether it is time to overhaul the entire business model.

One of the main hurdles in dealing with a failing or underperforming company is overcoming people's mental blocks that seriously limit the scope of strategic thinking. Such strategic inertia is a recipe for long-term decline because, when a company doesn't keep pace with external developments, its strategy drifts. It is essential to break out of the business-as-usual mindset and to open your thinking to possibilities. Competition doesn't stand still and neither should your business model.

The process of paradigm change

The following diagram outlines three stages of improving business performance. The first step involves tightening controls. The second step involves developing new strategies that are still aligned with the current paradigm. The third step involves changing the paradigm itself.

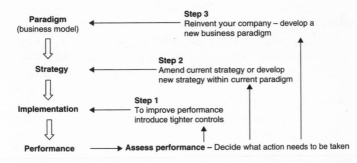

Crucially, this model is designed to improve business performance. It therefore starts with an existing model or paradigm, translated into a strategy which is then implemented. The opportunity and impetus to improve the business model becomes compelling only after the strategy has been implemented and the effects on performance are assessed. At that point the process of reinvention can gain pace starting with step 1 – the need for tighter controls – before moving to steps 2 and 3.

ANSOFF'S PRODUCT MATRIX

Getting from A to B

Ansoff's Product Matrix provides a useful means of clarifying your thinking through generating a snapshot of where you are and where you would like to be and enabling you to identify strategic priorities.

By helping you to see the gap between the current situation and your goals, the Product Matrix serves to illuminate your situation, your goals, your thinking and the route you need to take. Knowing your goal isn't enough: you need to know what needs to be done to get there. Strategy consists of two elements: portfolio strategy and competitive strategy. Portfolio strategy sets the goals for each product and market, while competitive strategy determines how to achieve those goals.

The grid

The grid has four areas that point to different options, depending on your current situation and goals.

	Current product	New product
Current market	Market penetration Increase market share	Product development Develop new products for existing markets
New market	Market development Take existing products into new markets	Diversification Develop entirely new products for new markets

The portfolio strategy explores each product and market combination as geographical growth vectors. These vectors have three aspects – market needs, market location and product needs (such as required technology). The three-dimensional nature of Ansoff's grid highlights the many points of intersection of current and potential products, market locations and market needs. By seeing how these aspects intersect, it will clarify the strategic options that are open to your company.

Ansoff's Product Matrix provides a clear snapshot to help you set and achieve strategic goals. There are four aspects to using the matrix that are all connected – the priorities you set in one will inevitably affect the others. The four aspects are:

1 **The geographical growth vector.** Know where you are and where you want to be. Assess your current product and market combinations and decide what and where you would like those combinations to be in the future.
2 **Competitive advantage.** Determine your core strengths and what gives you a competitive edge. Then identify the resources and capabilities needed to achieve goals – know what your company does well and not so well and the skills, resources and technology it will need to acquire.
3 **Synergies.** Identify synergies between activities, cut costs and bolster competitiveness.
4 **Flexibility.** Ensure that your company is prepared for the unexpected and is able to respond quickly and effectively to change. Make sure that one part of the company can incorporate change without harming other parts.

RESOURCES AND THE CRITICAL PATH

The drivers of business performance

'Resources' is an overused term in business but any factor providing value or benefit, from whatever origin, is a resource that can be used to benefit the business. Increasing and strengthening resources over time can be seen as the critical path to business success.

Managing resources

Assessing which resources are important involves taking a view across the whole of the business and identifying those factors, direct or indirect, tangible or intangible, that can be expanded and used for competitive advantage. Understanding which resources are most important and how they should be managed requires a clear understanding of the nature of each resource, in terms of the following:

- **The interaction between resources.** Resources can combine in a cycle to accelerate their growth. For example, rising sales volumes may lead to more cash and more internal capacity, both of which can be used to generate increasing sales, perhaps by entering new markets, in a self-sustaining cycle. Similarly, product quality (an intangible resource) may lead to increased sales, and this in turn can generate sufficient cash to continue improving product quality (and continue increasing sales). In the same way that resources can interact to reinforce one another, they can also interact by limiting one another.

- **The fragility of the resource.** Cash, quality, customers, staff, reputation and most other resources can all disappear with remarkable speed and ease. It is, therefore, important to control the main factors likely to damage or undermine resources. For example: cash needs to be monitored and controlled; quality can be eroded by suppliers; service can be undermined by the attitudes of personnel; and brand reputation may be damaged by the actions of distributors.

- **The quality of resources.** It is worth considering how the quality of resources can be developed. For example, a customer base is a valuable resource, but its quality might be improved by increasing customer loyalty to your brand – for instance, by using customer loyalty schemes.

How resources affect performance

Resources have a special characteristic: they fill and drain over time. Since a firm's performance at any time directly reflects the resources available, it is essential that we understand how those resources develop over time and how we can control that process. To build strong business performance, we need to know:

- how many resources are available
- how fast these numbers are changing
- how strongly these factors are being influenced by things under our control and by other forces
- how resources interrelate with one another.

In a system where resources are integrated and working together, what matters is not the uniqueness of individual resources but how they combine and work together to deliver value for customers. To manage resources and ensure that they drive performance in the desired direction, start by understanding how resources work together.

DEVELOPING INTANGIBLE RESOURCES

Intangibles: what they are, why they matter, and what they can do for you

Soft 'intangible' factors can play a crucial role in developing a business's competitive performance. For example, a charity with strong commitment from its donors will achieve its goals more easily, and a business with a culture that encourages coaching, risk-taking, new ideas and avoids blame is more likely to make improvements and achieve progress.

Unfortunately, intangibles can be tough to manage. You may easily borrow cash, buy production capacity or hire staff, but it is slow and difficult to build staff morale, a strong reputation, support from a charity's donors or to generate new ideas.

Overview

Resources can typically be classified into two of four categories: either direct or indirect and tangible or intangible.

- **Direct resources** are those factors such as staff expertise, cash or intellectual property that can be developed and nurtured by the business. Customers are, perhaps, the biggest single direct resource. (Viewing customers as a resource focuses thinking on how to accumulate and retain them.)
- **Indirect resources** are those factors that have a bearing on the quality, strength and value of resources. For example, effective training and development policies are an indirect resource, as they build the effectiveness of staff expertise.
- **Tangible resources** are those that can be physically seen, such as cash, inventory, sales volumes and customers; typically, these have the highest profile within the organization, as they are the most apparent.
- **Intangible resources** such as service quality, brand reputation or staff expertise are also vitally important to success.

Of these, intangible resources can be the hardest to manage (and the easiest to ignore). Several techniques will help ensure that intangible resources are working well with the rest of the business:

- **Identify the most important intangibles.** Since your performance relies on concrete resources, assess whether an intangible factor is likely to influence your ability to win or lose the resources. It is not advisable to waste time examining too many factors, as it is more likely that only one or two factors will have a significant impact.
- **Be clear which of these factors genuinely 'accumulate' through time** and which are simply current features of the business. 'Quality' and 'service' reflect the balance between what has to be done and what is available to do it, in which case they do not accumulate. Reputation, motivation, commitment and relationships, on the other hand, are built up and drain away over time in response to events.
- **Assess intangibles carefully,** identify the best measure and also the events causing each intangible to rise or fall. Look for ways to strengthen intangibles.
- **Build intangible measures into your performance tracking system.** Reporting systems now commonly incorporate soft measures (as distinct from hard data, such as financial measures) from various parts of the organization, recognizing that soft measures such as engagement or reputation are crucial to a well-performing system.
- **If you don't know, don't ignore the issue.** Soft factors are influencing your organization, continually and powerfully. Remember, if you choose to ignore them, you are not, in fact, really leaving them out. Instead, you are assuming that they are satisfactory and unchanging. This is unlikely to remain correct, so make your best estimate and start tracking and understanding them.

MARKET POSITIONING AND VALUE CURVES

Choosing the best position in the market for your business or product

A value curve is a way of highlighting customers' needs and preferences. This can be used to understand a firm's competitive position, as well as potential trade-offs, opportunities and areas for further development.

Competing firms emphasize and trade off different things that customers value. For example:

- The UK retailer **The Body Shop** traded the slick packaging, clinical approach and glamorous image traditionally favoured by the cosmetics industry in return for a lower price and a more sustainable identity (see diagram).
- In the USA **South-West Airlines** pioneered low-cost aviation by trading the features of traditional air travel in return for the benefits of cheap, point-to-point travel.
- **Multiplex cinemas** traded the conventional convenience and centrality of town centre locations in return for the benefits of space and a different experience for customers.
- **Home Depot** expanded into out-of-town locations on freeways and employed ex-contractors as a way of providing a new level of service and value for customers who did not typically visit home building stores.

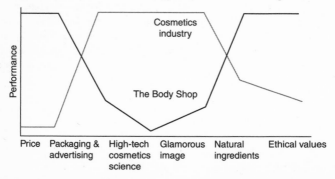

The concept of value curves highlights several points about market positioning:

- Competing firms emphasize and trade off different values (e.g. luxury may be traded for a lower price).
- Customers value specific features (e.g. price, packaging) differently at different times.
- Different values enable firms to target new, different – and possibly un-fulfilled – market segments, potentially increasing the size of the market.
- Initially, strategic innovators (e.g. South-West Airlines) create new 'market space', gradually redefining the market.
- It can be extremely difficult, if not impossible, for incumbents to successfully copy new arrivals. This is because internal cultural and resource issues keep firms anchored in their conventional way of working.
- When reviewing a value curve, consider the trend: how are things changing?

COMPETITIVE ANALYSIS: PORTER'S FIVE FORCES

How competitive is your company?

Porter's Five Forces model provides a deeper understanding of a firm's current competitiveness and highlights options to improve competitiveness.

Michael Porter outlines five forces for competitive analysis:

1 New entrants
2 Substitute products
3 Buyers
4 Suppliers
5 Existing competitors.

1 New entrants

Ask yourself how easy it is for new companies to enter the market. There are many factors to consider, including barriers to entry (such as patents and high set-up costs), attractiveness of profit margins and the strength of your brand.

2 Substitutes

Assess how easy it is for your products to be substituted by other products. This includes all alternatives – not just similar products. For example, airlines compete with train and coach companies, not just other airlines.

3 Buyers

Review how strong your buyers are. Is it a buyers' market? Can buyers switch to competitors easily? Are some of your customers in such a strong position that this leaves you vulnerable? If your business-to-business buyers are operating at low profit margins, what impact will this have on your company?

4 Suppliers

Assess the strength of your suppliers. Are you dependent on a particular supplier – and how can this be mitigated? Does the supplier rely on your custom or could it easily take its operating capacity to other companies or sell directly to your customers? Could you use alternative products or methods to reduce your vulnerability?

5 Existing competitors

Understand your competitors and how you compare to them.

- What threat do they pose?
- What are their strengths and weaknesses?
- Could there be a price war or other aggressive strategies – and would you be able to survive such tactics?
- Are they innovative?
- Are customers able to move to other companies easily?
- How many competitors are there?
- Which companies are the strongest?
- Are there any newcomers ready to take the market by storm or render your products redundant?

Assessing competitiveness through all five forces will help you to determine how the company is performing, its strengths and weaknesses and the direction it is heading in. Because a weakness of Porter's approach is the focus on external issues, it is often used alongside complementary models that are better at revealing the internal issues that impact on a company's competitiveness.

DEVELOPING INNOVATION AND CREATIVITY

INNOVATION HOTSPOTS

How to build a culture of innovation

Developed by Professor Lynda Gratton, Innovation Hotspots occur where conditions are right and there is encouragement – they cannot be formally imposed. Encouragement is needed in four areas, which are:

1 a co-operative mindset
2 boundary spanning
3 developing a sense of purpose
4 productive capacity.

1 A co-operative mindset

A co-operative mindset results from a company's practices, processes, behaviours and norms – the behaviour of top management is significant. People have to want to share both explicit and tacit knowledge. Several elements are vital:

- Consider relationships when selecting staff.
- Emphasize relationships in inductions.
- Provide mentoring.
- Emphasize collective rewards over individual ones.
- Establish structures that facilitate peer-to-peer working.
- Develop social responsibility.

2 Boundary spanning

This involves thinking beyond your immediate boundaries – seeing the larger picture. This involves:

- being undeterred by physical distance
- welcoming a diverse range of ideas, insights, experience and people
- being willing and able to explore issues together
- networking and building bridges for others to cross

- using different levels of co-operation (e.g., use strong ties where developing trust quickly is important; use weak ties to generate a lot of ideas)
- listening and reflecting in conversations rather than just pushing a point of view.

3 Developing a sense of purpose

Pose challenging (or 'igniting') questions. These don't have a 'right' answer; they invite exploration of options. They inspire and engage people and lead to a new vision that provides purpose and energy.

4 Productive capacity

Ensuring that a hotspot realizes its full potential relies on building productive capacity by:

- understanding and appreciating the talents of others
- obtaining practical, public and explicit commitment from participants
- harnessing the creative energy which results from problem-solving and decision-making
- synchronizing time, especially where different time zones have to be accommodated or where there are different attitudes to time
- ensuring that pressure is neither too high, where people burn out, or too low, where they lose interest.

Innovation relies on teamwork, agility and the ability to lead change. Crucially, it is about mindset: you need to think like an innovator and you need to encourage this in others. Innovation isn't only about products – it's about understanding customers and building a brand, improving efficiency, reducing costs, improving the quality and quantity of people's work and removing constraints.

DEEP DIVE PROTOTYPING

Developing creative, practical solutions

Developed and popularized by the consultancy firm IDEO, Deep Dive Prototyping is a focused, team-based approach to generating solutions to a particular problem or challenge. It is a useful way of stimulating creative thinking and to capture and fine-tune ideas.

The process

A deep dive combines brainstorming and prototyping (building and exploring a potential solution) to devise actions that will help move a business forward. There is no time limit, and the main stages are:

- Build a team that has a mix of strengths and approaches.
- Define the design challenge – to do this, understand your market, customers, technology and constraints and use this information to develop key themes.
- Visit experts, and gather information on markets, customers – and ideas generally.
- Share ideas.
- Brainstorm and vote – this involves intensive brainstorming and discussion to imagine new concepts and ideas based around the main themes.
- Develop a fast prototype.
- Test and refine the prototype, streamlining ideas to improve the prototype and to overcome obstacles – at this stage, evaluate and prioritize ideas and decide how they can be implemented.
- Focus on the prototype and produce a final solution.
- Give credit to those involved – this promotes motivation and encourages continued innovative thinking.

DEVELOPING CREATIVE THINKING

Making creativity the norm

Edward de Bono sees creativity as a learnable skill, one that is best harnessed through formal techniques. He proposes that parallel thinking is a more useful and effective means of putting creative talent to work.

Formal creativity works because it works with the way everyone's brains work: both consciously and subconsciously, we automatically filter, categorize, process and organize information. Building on this, de Bono argues that parallel thinking is more effective for generating the results that make a difference to companies. (Parallel thinking is when each individual puts forward their own thoughts *in parallel* with those of others. In this way, each individual is able to complement, enrich and build on one another's thinking, rather than competing or attacking the thoughts of others.)

The reason why this is more important than ever is because what companies previously relied on for competitive advantage – competence, information and technology – are now easy-to-obtain commodities. These are all buyable commodities, enabling your competitors to rapidly erode any advantage you may have had. Today, what matters is creating value from these commodities.

Understanding creativity

Creativity solves problems, challenges existing methods, and provides a better and constantly improving way forward. Given the reward, companies need to know how best to harness creativity in a way that is useful. A major flaw in traditional brainstorming is that it assumes that, if you give people the freedom to express themselves, they will magically become creative. This is not the case. For organizations, useful creativity needs to be a formal activity that requires thinking that provokes and challenges a current situation and then searches for answers.

Provoke, challenge and search for solutions

Given the brain's natural inclination to organize information and think laterally, we can tackle issues by simply taking a random starting point. Our brains will automatically process information, make connections and point us in new directions. Allowing such randomness in selecting a starting point is important. It suggests new possibilities and takes thinking along new paths. Significantly, it is likely that our brains have already processed information and are subconsciously suggesting such opening gambits because they could be highly relevant. This serves to break us out of the current doldrums and set us on a new course.

Next, our new thinking needs to move forward: to challenge the information it is processing. Just because something has always been done a certain way does not mean it is carved in stone: methods can *always* be improved upon. Constantly questioning and challenging is a mindset that is a huge source of competitive advantage precisely because it is the way that companies create value from their resources. An important point to remember is that even when something seems to be working and is successful it doesn't mean it is the best that it can be. Once thinking challenges the norm, we will automatically explore alternative and potentially better solutions.

Creating a culture of creativity in a world where competence, knowledge and technology are no longer enough is now the true source of success.

THE DISCOVERY CYCLE (ORCA)

Evaluating innovations

Discovery – making things known or visible – is a vital precursor for innovation. The Discovery Cycle is a way of choosing new ideas that are profitable and scalable.

The Discovery Cycle has four stages, summarized in the acronym ORCA:

1 **Observation.** Understand how the world is changing – for example, by looking for anomalies, paradoxes, peripheral developments and direct experience.
2 **Reflection.** Techniques that work best at this stage include zooming in and out, using a muse, suspending judgement, slowing down, reflecting on what's missing, restructuring data to simplify patterns, juxtaposing pieces of different information (bisociation) and taking time to rest.
3 **Conversation.** People set the pace and scope for innovation, so the best techniques to use at this stage include contrasting views, setting the agenda, framing the issues and generating hypotheses.
4 **Analysis.** The final stage of the Discovery Cycle involves gathering systematic evidence, classifying and categorizing data, naming, completing data analysis and hypothesizing.

Lessons from great innovators

What lessons do innovators have for us? Several come to mind:

- Build on the ideas of others / collaborate. That should be easy for scientists who are, in the words of Isaac Newton, 'standing on the shoulders of giants'.
- Take an unorthodox, distinctive approach.
- Embrace diversity.
- Create a diverse, open and creative culture.
- Develop empathy for the consumer or customer (understand people).
- Execute and practically take action.
- Be confident and bold.
- Find your motivation; enjoy your work.

This list also highlights three other vital points:

1 Innovation relies on teamwork, agility and the ability to lead change, the other elements of this programme.
2 Innovation is about mindset: you need to think like an innovator and you need to encourage that in others.
3 Innovation isn't only about products: it is about improving efficiency, reducing costs, improving the quality and quantity of people's work, removing constraints – and that's just internally; it also means serving and understanding customers, building a brand – and more.

THE FORTUNE AT THE BOTTOM OF THE PYRAMID (BOP)

Developing the innovator's mindset

If a company goes to the bottom of the wealth pyramid and builds affordable products, creates awareness and provides access, then the market is phenomenal.

The late Professor C.K. Prahalad argued that there is a 'poverty penalty' where the poorest people pay more for everything because they don't have a choice: they are stuck with local monopolies and bad products and services.

Research recently highlighted by the World Resources Institute shows that the world's four billion poorest people represent a US$5 trillion market opportunity. There are several other issues at the bottom of the pyramid:

- **Pricing is vital.** At the BOP, you need to start with an affordable price, understanding that price minus profit equals the acceptable level of cost. This different way of thinking leads to a new range of exciting options.
- **Innovation is essential.** This can be accelerated and improved by focusing on BOP markets because minor, incremental changes won't be enough: the market requires a fundamental rethink.
- **Businesses need to substitute investment for collaboration.** Management time is needed to increase collaboration – and it is cheaper than simply investing cash.

Companies that ignore growth markets will be left behind – and will have five years, at best, before businesses from growth markets start competing with them.

Developing the innovator's mindset

Where can you improve your approach to innovation? Ask yourself the following questions and mark yourself out of 10 for each attribute: this will help highlight areas for improvement.

When innovating, how effectively do you:

- engage as many people as possible …? ☐
- … and build an open, diverse and positive team? ☐
- define the specific challenge or issue? ☐
- challenge assumptions: yours and other people's? ☐
- confront challenges and problems? ☐
- understand that good ideas can come from anywhere? ☐

- follow through – by being practical and realistic, and planning implementation? ☐
- focus on the benefits as well as the potential pitfalls? ☐
- question? Questioning is a great way both to provide support (e.g. what help do you need?) and challenge (how can we do this faster/cheaper?) ☐
- give praise and credit: build momentum (revolutions fail, flywheels succeed)? ☐
- be open, build relationships? ☐
- remove constraints, tirelessly? ☐
- remember the essentials of leading change? (See Number 35.) ☐
- balance intuition and analysis? ☐
- build collaboration and teamwork? (Think of the 5Ms: meaning, mindset, measurement, mobilizing, mechanisms for renewal.) ☐
- avoid the pitfalls of decision-making? (See the description of inhibitors below – which ones are your greatest vulnerability?) ☐
- consciously develop your skills? ☐
- design matters? (This affects how people feel about something: whether it's credible, engaging, worthwhile.) ☐

The inhibitors of creative thinking are shown in this table.

Personal blocks	Problem-solving blocks	Contextual blocks
• Lack of self-confidence	• Solution fixedness	• Scientific reasoning provides a panacea
• A tendency to conform	• Premature judgement	• Resistance to new ideas
• A need for the familiar	• Use of poor approaches	• Isolation
• Emotional 'numbness'	• Lack of disciplined effort	• Negativity towards creative thinking
• Saturation	• Experts	• Excessive enthusiasm
• Poor language skills	• Autocratic decision-making	• Lack of imaginative control
• Rigidity	• Overemphasis on competition or co-operation	• Lack of smart goals, clear vision or timescale

THE SIX THINKING HATS

If you want to get ahead, get a hat

Created by Edward de Bono, the Six Thinking Hats technique details the different styles of thinking that we use when making decisions.

Overview

People tend to have a preferred thinking style which, no matter how useful, can overlook solutions to problems that would only be revealed through other ways of thinking. The Six Thinking Hats method gives us the flexibility either to use the style that is appropriate to a situation or the ability to gain a fuller picture by applying more than one thinking style to a problem.

Each thinking hat represents a different way of thinking. By seeing situations from these different perspectives, you are more likely to make and implement the right decision. For example, seeing a strategy only from a logical and rational perspective may result in a failure to see a better solution or potential obstacles to implementation that creative and sensitive thinking could reveal.

The Six Thinking Hats

- **White hat.** This approach focuses on available data. It involves looking at the information you have to see what you can learn from it – identifying gaps in your knowledge and, by analysing past trends and data, trying either to fill them or take account of them.
- **Red Hat.** This style looks at problems using intuition, gut reaction and emotion. Try to think how other people will react emotionally and try to understand the responses of people who don't know, or may not share, your reasoning.
- **Black Hat.** This looks at all the bad points of an issue, looking for why it won't work. It highlights the weak points in a plan, enabling you to eliminate or change them or to prepare contingency plans – helping to make plans more resilient. A key strength of this approach is that problems can be anticipated and countered.

- **Yellow Hat.** This style involves positive thinking and optimism, helping you to see the benefits of a decision. Another advantage is that it enables you to keep going during difficult situations.
- **Green Hat.** This involves developing creative solutions. Thinking is free-wheeling, and there is little criticism of ideas.
- **Blue Hat.** This emphasizes control of processes and is common among those chairing meetings. When ideas are running dry, it is useful to combine this approach with Green Hat thinking, as its creative approach will stimulate fresh ideas.

INNOVATION CULTURE

Peter Drucker's seven steps for developing a creative culture

Innovation is a company-wide activity. Creative, profitable ideas are needed to succeed, and history has shown us that great ideas come from many different people. Instead of relying on ad hoc suggestions or the skills of a few talented individuals, companies need to create an innovative culture.

Where does innovation come from?

While some people are known for their innovative thinking, successful and profitable ideas can come from anyone. To tap into this potential, what is needed is a culture that empowers people to question and think critically and creatively and then to share their ideas with others.

Innovation is not a rarefied activity or the domain of specialists. Neither is it solely about making huge leaps in thinking – smaller, incremental improvements are also significant sources of advantage. Innovation is not necessarily about large R&D budgets – important new ideas come from anywhere, at any time. It is a company-wide activity, reaching every aspect of running a business – from products and services to operations, decision-making and training. They are all sources of competitive advantage, and having an innovative culture will lead to continual improvements.

Creating an innovative organization

What distinguishes an innovative company from the rest is its dedication to creativity. Having the right culture and processes will lead to creative thinking, a challenging mindset and innovation. Innovative companies develop a creative culture where people challenge, innovate and look for opportunities. They adapt structures and procedures to enable innovation to flourish. Also, they often link with external experts to add to internal, innovative resources.

Peter Drucker outlines seven steps that promote innovation in a company:

1 Analyse the reasons for unexpected successes.
2 Examine why events were different from anticipated results.
3 Challenge the status quo by examining why underperformance has become an accepted state.
4 Determine how to take advantage of market changes.
5 Be aware of broader developments in society, to identify potential opportunities.
6 Consider the impact of changes in the economy and recognize the business opportunities they may offer.
7 Think about how new information, ideas and technology affect customers.

Innovative organizations also have a general environment and culture that values and fosters innovation. Research by the Talent Foundation identified five catalysts for successful innovation:

1 **Consciousness.** Each person knows the goals of the organization and believes that they can play a part in achieving them.
2 **Multiplicity.** Teams and groups contain a wide and creative mix of skills, experiences, backgrounds and ideas.
3 **Connectivity.** Relationships are strong and trusting and are actively encouraged and supported within and across teams and functions.
4 **Accessibility.** Doors and minds are open; everyone in the organization has access to resources, time and decision-makers.
5 **Consistency.** Commitment to innovation runs throughout the organization and is built into processes and leadership style.

If you are building an innovation culture in your business or team, it can help to ask yourself which of these catalysts you can improve. How will you do this?

DISNEY'S CREATIVITY STRATEGY

When you need more than just the bare necessities

We all have a preferred thinking style – some of us are dreamers, while others are realists or critics. This can prevent us seeing an issue from other angles. Walt Disney's method uses all three of these thinking styles to help view a situation from different perspectives and find the best way forward.

Problem solving, decision-making and planning suffer when we have too narrow a focus, yet it can be difficult to change how we naturally approach issues. Using Disney's three styles together will improve your decision-making.

- **The Dreamer**, who is a dreamer, is focused on potential and possibilities.
- **The Realist** focuses on practical aspects and implementation.
- **The Critic** questions and challenges plans and assumptions, and notices potential problems or flaws.

Using the Disney method

1 Select an issue you want to address but put it to one side while you get into the right frame of mind.
2 Go to three different places to think about the issue from each perspective (you will associate each environment with that approach). These can be entirely different places or simply different parts of one room.
3 For each way of thinking (starting with dreamer, moving to realistic and then to critic), first remember a time when you were either creative, realistic or critical. This will help you access that style and apply it to the current situation.
4 In each frame of mind, address the issue at hand solely from that perspective. This will let you get the most out of each perspective, revealing more options and ideas.
   - In the dreamer space, let your ideas flow freely.
   - In the realist space, think about how the ideas you have created can be implemented. How can they be achieved? What needs to happen?

- In the critic space, question and challenge your ideas and plan. Identify strengths and weaknesses; look for flaws; look for gaps or potential problems. Determine what needs to be done better.
5 Once you have completed these four stages, go back to the beginning and re-evaluate your original dream and plan through each thinking stage in turn. You can repeat this process until you feel the plan works well from each perspective.

Types of questions to ask at each stage

Dreamer	Realist
• Why am I doing this?	• How can I make that happen?
• Can it be done better?	• Who else do I need to make it work?
• What would I like to happen?	• What needs to happen – and when?
• Wouldn't it be great if ...?	• What resources do I need?
• What reward or result would I like?	• How much will it cost?
Critic	
• Does the idea really have potential?	
• Is the objective achievable?	
• Are there any barriers or resource issues?	
• Does the plan work? Consider issues such as timing, cost or market potential.	
• How can the plan be improved – are there gaps or are some things unnecessary?	

SALES, MARKETING, BRANDING AND CUSTOMER SERVICE

THE MATE MODEL FOR STRATEGIC SELLING

Achieving your sales objectives

Segmenting and managing your contacts within a client organization in terms of their support for your sales objectives is a highly effective way of developing client relationships and selling.

Four steps

- Step 1: define your unique sales objective.
- Be clear about what you are selling and when, and the value it brings. What makes it an attractive proposition? What is its value for the organization or client? This sounds simple but it can be muddled or overlooked, with disastrous consequences.
- Step 2: identify all the players using the MATE model.
- MATE highlights the need to focus on Money, Allies, Technical experts and End users. Identify each contact (including those you don't know), recording their job title and name.

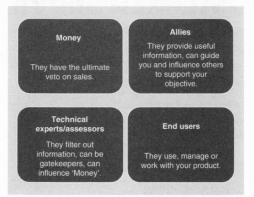

- **Money.** The budget holder has authority over the decision to spend. They tend to focus on the bottom line and have the power of veto. They will ask: 'What impact will this have and what return will we get?'

- **Allies / Advocates.** These can help guide you during the sales process. They provide valuable information, can lead you to the right people and may be influential. Allies are both inside and outside the organization.
- **Technical experts.** They are gatekeepers who evaluate technical aspects of the proposal. They do not have final approval but offer recommendations to the decision-maker. They can say 'no' on account of technical issues. They ask whether the product or service matches their specifications.
- **End users.** They judge the impact of your proposal on their job performance. They will implement or work with your solution, so their success is linked to your product and they will want to influence the decision to buy. They ask: Will it work for me or my department?
- Step 3: consider each individual's level of support.
- Having placed each individual on the MATE model, assess their level of support for your sales objective as high, medium or low.
- Step 4: consider each individual's level of influence.
- Assess each individual's influence within their organization – high, medium or low.

Check for warning signs

Ensure that there are no threats to the sale by asking yourself the following:

- Have I at least one person for each area?
- Am I free from concerns about their influence?
- Have I made personal contact with them?
- Do I know their response modes and what they are looking for?

Identify your tactics to further the sale and eliminate warning signs

Throughout, be honest and prepared to challenge and develop your thinking. With the information you have gathered, contact the key people, establish rapport and understand their needs.

THE TEN CS OF SELLING ONLINE

Building a successful business online

Centred round meeting customers' needs, the Ten Cs are the key drivers of selling and succeeding with business online. Which factors are most significant for your company will vary over time, depending on the situation – such as its stage of development, competitive position, type of market or brand strength.

1 Content

Content sets the tone and should drive your brand. It should be clear, compelling, engaging, entertaining, informative, visually appealing and tailored to the target audience. Enable customers to access information quickly and easily and to control the flow of information.

2 Communication

Communication is more than providing information. It is about listening, building trust and having a one-to-one relationship with customers. Understand what interests and motivates customers, give them the opportunity to interact, act on feedback and use clickstream data to monitor behaviour.

3 Customer care

Customers need to trust you – to have confidence in purchases and to know that personal data is secure and that after-sales support is available. Provide various payment methods, enable customers to track orders and respond quickly to questions. Positive experiences enable up-selling, cross-selling, repeat business and personal recommendations.

4 Community and culture

People look to the Internet to network and socialize. Provide expert information, allow people to react, ensure that information is accessible, clear and entertaining, and enable customers to meet and interact.

5 Convenience

Customers have high expectations, so assess each feature from your customers' viewpoint. Online experiences need to be smooth, effective, quick, easy and convenient. Ensure that navigation is clear and intuitive.

6 Connectivity

Make the site compelling and 'sticky' – so that customers stay longer, return often and recommend it. Ensure that customers value it by providing high-quality content and incentives to return. Enable customers to visit other sites that provide complementary information – such as skiing companies linking to weather channels.

7 Cost and profitability

Your online strategy – objectives, priorities and benefits – needs to be clearly understood and planned. Focus on cost control and profit maximization to ensure that the site is profitable.

8 Customization

Plan customization from the outset rather than grafting it on later. Ensure that products meet customer's requirements through dialogue. Make sure that customers know what they can and cannot choose. Develop and refine customization to maintain competitiveness.

9 Capability

To improve capabilities, encourage your people to see the Internet as a tool for meeting customer needs. Set, implement, measure and monitor objectives. Ask customers what they want and what they think of your plans.

10 Competitiveness

Continually review and refine your strategy relative to competitors. You need a keen market awareness – you need to know what competitors have done, are doing and may do. Consider the worst-case scenario to make your online strategy durable and realistic.

SEVEN STEPS TO SUCCESSFUL SALES MEETINGS

From great rapport to a sale

Successful sales meetings are critical. This is true for both sides: your company's future depends on sales, and clients want to find the right supplier. Selling is a highly skilled art, one that is rooted in one fundamental principle: trust.

Overview

These seven steps will help you to make the difference and turn sales meetings into a win-win for all concerned. Each step provides an invaluable framework to building the right relationship with your potential clients – skills that can be used in a wide range of business situations.

Step 1	Build rapport	Connect with you the client – establish common ground and empathize.
		Create a positive working relationship and remain professional.
		Be warm and assertive and ask open questions.
		Dress to establish credibility.
Step 2	Send confirmation of your purpose	Be clear, concise and appealing.
		This shows why the meeting is important, establishes your capability and enables you take to control.
Step 3	Introduce yourself and your company	Your client needs to have confidence in you and your company. Your ability to direct the rest of the meeting relies on this first impression.
		Be succinct and aim to impress – include how you have helped other companies. Use positive, non-committal words such as 'hopefully' and 'possibilities'.

Step 4	Fact-finding	This helps you to know your potential client and tailor your offer. This includes knowing both the company's situation and the people you are meeting with – ensure that your presentation appeals to and resonates with those listening.
Step 5	Explore needs and wants	This is where sales are made or lost. Focus on their needs and what they are looking for. If you want to include things they haven't previously considered, give a compelling reason. Explain how what you are offering will make a difference to their business.
		Use GRIP: Goals, Reality, Implications, Plans (see Chapter 59). Focus on what they are looking for and value. Ask open, probing questions – and listen. Don't be afraid of silence – people need time to think about points.
Step 6	The presentation	Tailor your presentation to what the client needs. It is no good having bells and whistles if they are of no use to your client.
		Be enthusiastic and warm and tie your solution to the client's needs.
Step 7	Advancing and closing	All previous steps rely on this last stage.
		End meetings by focusing on building the relationship.
		Agree next steps and reaffirm commitment.
		Be confident and warm, follow up quickly and deliver on promises.

THE BUYER'S CYCLE

Understanding how customers buy

Successful selling requires understanding of how and why people buy. By understanding each stage of the Buyer's Cycle, you will be able to influence current and potential customers.

Empathy and seeing situations from a client's point of view is fundamental. Customers think about three things:

1 their current situation
2 how your product will affect that situation
3 whether it will close a gap and take them closer to their goals.

When selling to an organization, the different people involved can have different views and priorities.

How the Buyer's Cycle works

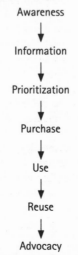

Awareness

↓

Information

↓

Prioritization

↓

Purchase

↓

Use

↓

Reuse

↓

Advocacy

1 **Awareness.** Catch the customer's attention – make them curious about and familiar with your product. Create awareness of your product so as to lead the customer to the next stage: wanting to know more.

2 **Information.** Make information clear, useful, relevant and compelling, with the right amount of detail for the customer. Too much will be irrelevant, tedious and boring for some; too little will lack the necessary detail for others. The information and how you present it will lead the customer towards prioritizing their needs in relation to your product.

3 **Prioritization.** This is when decisions are made. Understand your customer's needs, 'would like to haves', their situation and financial concerns. Essentially, help them find the product that is right for them. Without this, the advocacy stage will not occur –they will not recommend you to others.

4 **Purchase.** Make the process of buying as simple, streamlined and efficient as possible. If the process is tedious or complicated, the sale may fall through. This applies to both business-to-business and business-to-consumer selling. Ensure that customers are pleased with their purchases.

5 **Use.** The sale is not the end of the selling process. How customers use products affects repeat business and recommendations. Provide good products, generous guarantees and great after-sales support to move customers to the next two stages: reuse and advocacy.

6 **Reuse.** Repeat customers are lucrative. They are high-margin customers, requiring little marketing spend to increase revenue. Also, they recommend your product to others through personal and career contacts and social media.

7 **Advocacy.** It is called the Buyer's *Cycle* for a reason: advocacy leads directly back to the awareness stage. Recommendations reduce the cost and difficulty of gaining other customers. To potential customers, a recommendation brings a product to their attention, removes uncertainty and builds a desire to own it.

PRICING

Choosing the best strategy

Getting the price right from the outset is imperative: the wrong price can undermine your whole business strategy. Once set, prices can be difficult to change.

Price supports a range of business aims: increasing loyalty, prolonging a product's lifespan, entering new markets, manipulating special offers and driving out competition. To choose a pricing strategy you need in-depth understanding of markets, customers, strategic aims and your company.

Know how sensitive price is

Is demand elastic – where small changes in price lead to significant changes in demand? Or is it inelastic – where changes in price have little effect on demand? Does the product have 'snob' value, where demand increases with high prices?

Know the market

What are customer perceptions and behaviour? Will you accept the pricing culture – or challenge it?

Competitive issues and price innovation

Are there few direct competitors? Are some competitors vulnerable to lower prices?

Costs and break-even analysis

Selling at cost establishes market share or drives out competitors – break-even analysis determines the price that covers costs. Review all costs, including the possibility of suppliers increasing prices.

Pricing strategies

Strategy	Idea/aim	Issues
Loss leading	Price is less than cost Remove competitors or establish market share	If demand is too high, losses escalate. Difficult to increase prices later. Could you survive a price war?
Penetration pricing	Break-even price and aggressive marketing Market penetration and gaining market share	Used in very competitive markets and to undermine established leader Relies on unit costs falling as demand rises Risk of competitors reducing prices
Milking or skimming	Premium price for high-quality version To generate further profit from established product	Return limited by higher costs of supplying product Relies on ability to convince customers Small size of market
Target pricing	Set minimum level of profit, estimate sales then set price	Relies on accurate sales estimates Failing to account for competitors' actions

(*Continued*)

PRICING

Strategy	Idea/aim	Issues
Price differentiation	Variable prices for different markets	Generates the most revenue from a product
		Relies on barriers to entry – e.g. tariffs or high costs – to prevent others buying in cheaper markets and reselling
		Relies on consumer ignorance (or acceptance) of cheaper prices elsewhere.
Marginal cost pricing	Price reflects additional cost of supplying extra unit	Used when cost of extra unit is significantly higher
		Need to explain price differences to customers
Variable pricing	Prices reduced, to increase sales	Often used in extreme situations
	Raised, to deter sales – if production at capacity	Price fluctuations risk alienating or confusing customers
Average cost pricing	Set base price by adding total costs and desired profit margin and dividing by likely sales	Accepted by customers
		Relies on accurate estimates
		Is competitive: companies with lowest costs charge lowest prices
Customary pricing	Same price for smaller product	Can increase profits
		Useful when costs are rising and demand is slow
		Risks alienating customers

Strategy	Idea/aim	Issues
Barrier pricing	Reduce prices to deter or remove new entrants	Aggressive strategy to defend established position
		Used in highly competitive or price-sensitive markets
		Despite legal restrictions, companies act together to maintain barrier pricing

THE FOUR PS OF MARKETING

Using the marketing mix

The marketing mix includes Product, Place, Price and Promotion and this can be used to successfully position a product in the market.

Edmund Jerome McCarthy framed the marketing mix as the Four Ps. While it may look simple, the point is that marketing is more than a reactive enterprise, responding to a product after it has been developed. It should also be a proactive activity that informs every aspect of a product's design and development.

Applying the Four Ps is a rigorous and ongoing process that questions and challenges every aspect of a product to improve the product offering – to get the marketing mix right. Each part affects the others (both supporting and potentially undermining), necessitating a co-ordinated approach to marketing strategy and the need to embed marketing into all other aspects of the business – from product design to strategic direction. By considering marketing issues from the start, you are more likely to develop the right products and then to get those products right.

Product: designing the products that customers want

- Understand customers – what do they want, how will they use the product, how the product will be perceived, what level of after-sales support will they expect?
- Consider the effect of costs on price and, as a consequence, on customers.
- Use market and customer insight to inform the product's features – including its name, attributes, colour, size and any relevant attributes.
- Get branding right, along with differentiating it from competitors' products.

Place: reaching customers

- Be clear about where and how products will reach customers – for example, the channels, regions and segments where they will be marketed and sold.
- Understand your customers – where they look for products and where they make purchases.
- You need to determine the channels you will use and consider distribution issues – including any barriers to entry.

Price: setting the right price

- Know what the customer will be prepared to pay and consider how customers' perceptions are guided by price.
- Decide a price that allows for discounts to be used effectively – such as encouraging bulk sales at a price that does not fall below costs.
- Be aware of competitors' prices and consider the potential for a price war.
- You will need to consider how demand will be affected at different prices.
- Ensure that the price does not needlessly sacrifice your profit margin.
- Consider price from other perspectives such as branding.

Promotion: making people aware of the product and enticing them to buy

- Decide how and when to appeal to customers.
- Know which type of promotion and incentive (for example, buy one get one free) would work best for particular customers.
- To plan a successful advertising campaign, you will need to know your customers. For example: Where do they go (and when)? What do they do? What do they read? What (and who) influences them?
- Be aware of competitors' campaigns and improve upon them.

THE TEN RULES OF CROSS-SELLING

Improving profitability

Cross-selling is offering one or more different products or services to a customer who has already made a purchase. The potential for increased profit is considerable, but mishandling the process can be self-defeating in the long term or even risk the original sale.

Overview

Successful cross-selling depends on understanding customer behaviour and how customers make decisions. The key is to focus completely on the customer. Fundamentally, honesty, integrity and trustworthiness are the hallmarks of successful cross-selling. To have real benefit, always keep in mind that you are aiming to increase profitability by building long-term relationships, encouraging customer recommendations and developing a valued brand – none of this will happen if customers are sold the wrong products or feel misguided in any way.

Applying the ten rules

To guide companies in using the process successfully and avoiding the pitfalls, John Domanski devised ten rules of cross-selling:

1 **Don't cross-sell too soon.** Do not risk losing the customer completely by cross-selling too soon – make sure the first purchase is finalized.
2 **Stick to the rule of 25,** where the value of the cross-sale does not increase the original order by more than 25 per cent.
3 **Focus on long-term profit.** Cross-selling needs to offer a customer the most suitable product or service and so build a long-term relationship and encourage personal recommendations. Simply pushing high-margin items is ultimately unprofitable because disappointed customers will not return.
4 **Add value for customers, always.** Cross-selling is not a means of disposing of unwanted stock – it is about adding value for customers.

5 **Keep all items in the sale connected.** From the customer's perspective, additional products or services must be related to the first item.

6 **Sell the customer something they already know:** offer additional products or services that the customer is already familiar with. This is not the time to introduce new products or services.

7 **Use technology to understand the customer.** Develop a system that links items together so that, when a customer makes a purchase, the list of cross-selling opportunities is immediately apparent. It then becomes a question of offering items that are appropriate to each particular customer.

8 **Keep sales teams as well as customers informed about products.** Sales teams need to know all your products and services thoroughly. Detailed understanding is needed to know which products to offer and to handle customers' questions.

9 **Use your best people and ensure continuous improvement.** When introducing new cross-selling opportunities, use your best people to test the process and improve how it works.

10 **Incentivize your sales teams to cross-sell** (it is still cost-effective). Always remember that motivation and compensation affect the performance of sales teams. Co-opting Einstein's equation, $E = M C^2$ sums this up, where E is the person's effort, M is the level of motivation and C is the amount of compensation – effort directly following better compensation and motivation speaks for itself.

DIFFERENTIATION

Giving customers a reason to choose your products

Differentiating one product from another creates new market opportunities: allowing variable pricing, increasing profit margins and distinguishing your products from competitors'. Differentiation takes many forms – from a product's features, price and reliability to emotional, aspirational attributes and branding.

Overview

In markets awash with products and services, getting customers to recognize and choose your products is difficult. Differentiating from competitors gives customers a reason to choose your product rather than a competitor's, and making this choice easy for customers is important.

Like it or not, our brains are remarkably lazy and prefer to make decisions with the least effort. This is not to say we are not fussy – clearly, we need to be convinced about the value the differentiation offers. However, the point is that differentiation itself prompts the customer into seeing a difference and helps to narrow down the decision-making process – in other words, it makes things easier. So, it is important to make your customers aware of how your product is different.

How to differentiate your products

- **Know your strengths and weaknesses – and your competitors'.** By understanding your own strengths and weaknesses, and those of your competitors, you will know what attributes you can leverage and what you need to do differently in order to outcompete rivals and to appeal to customers.
- **Focus on customers.** Differentiation strategy needs a keen focus on customers. Knowing what will appeal to them and how they will respond to any developments or changes in tastes and attitudes should always

inform your strategy – including recognizing new customer groups and opportunities.

- **Compete with yourself.** Many companies offer products that compete with their own products. By offering differentiated products, you will appeal to a broader range of customers and occupy a larger portion of the entire market, restricting the space available for competitors.

- **Be aware of shifts in the marketplace.** Differentiation is never a static situation. Competitors will copy your products or services and erode any advantage you once had. They will also use differentiation to capture your customers. You will need to continually scan the marketplace to assess competitors and to identify new opportunities.

CURRY'S PYRAMID FOR MARKETING AND CUSTOMER RELATIONSHIP MANAGEMENT

Segmenting, understanding and managing customers

How much do you invest in courting customers? The answer should depend on the profit they create. Curry's Pyramid provides a clear summary of your most valuable customers (and unprofitable ones) so that you can target your money, efforts and strategy accordingly.

Without customer segmentation, companies risk: wasting resources on loss-making customers; missing opportunities to increase profit through other customers; and alienating their most profitable ones. Curry's Pyramid helps to identify each group, clarify your thinking and determine your marketing and customer-relationship strategies – identifying groups to cross-sell and up-sell to.

The
top 1%

The next 4%
of customers

The next 15% of
customers

The next 80% of customers

Inactive customers – made past
purchases but not recently

Prospective customers – those that have
expressed an interest in your product

Suspects – those that haven't heard of your product
or company but may be interested in it

The basis of Curry's Pyramid is the revenue each customer group generates. It works from the 80/20 rule, where 20 per cent of the customers generate 80 per cent of the revenue, and 80 per cent of the customers provide 20 per cent of the revenue. This means:

- taking good care of the top 20 per cent of customers
- moving customers in lower-revenue-generating segments up the value chain
- understanding your reasons for marketing to low-profit segments
- questioning why you keep loss-making customers.

The pyramid can reflect different things – not simply revenue. It could depict profit margin per segment. Viewing groups solely in terms of revenue or profit margins is only part of the story – other factors need to be considered, such as brand and market presence. Nonetheless, given that a small customer group generates the bulk of your revenue and is probably highly profitable, Curry's Pyramid is useful for analysing customers and developing marketing strategy.

In practice

Decide how you are going to segment customers – for example, by revenue generation or profit margin per customer.

1 Collate and analyse the data.
2 Use this information to review and inform your marketing strategy.
3 Incorporate broader strategic aims into marketing strategy. Don't just focus on the now: consider potential customers (move customers up the value chain and turn prospective customers into actual ones).
4 Determine the levels of marketing costs that each segment justifies and develop tactics that are cost-sensitive and tied to revenue.
5 Take very good care of your most profitable customers.

Finally, Curry's Pyramid is designed to achieve one aim: to ensure that your company is customer-driven. If you are not focused 100 per cent on customers, then you are looking in the wrong direction.

THE TIPPING POINT

Malcolm Gladwell's insights into the way ideas spread

The emergence, spread and decline of products or ideas is a phenomenon that is rarely understood. Gladwell's insight into social dynamics, however, reveals the trends of human behaviour.

Malcolm Gladwell likens the rapid growth, decline and coincidence of ideas to epidemics. Ideas are 'infectious', fashions represent 'outbreaks' and new ideas and products are 'viruses' – and advertising is a way of infecting others. He shows how a factor tips when a critical mass is reached. This is when a shoe becomes a fashion craze, social smoking becomes addiction and crime becomes a wave. The idea of the 'tipping point' provides insight into how to launch products successfully.

1 The law of the few

Epidemics need a small number of people to transmit their infection to many others – those who travel and socialize can turn a local outbreak into a global pandemic. For business, word of mouth is critical. Those who speak the most (and are influential) create epidemics of ideas. These people are connectors, mavens and salespeople.

- **Connectors** bring people together. They influence the spread of epidemics through their networks. Masters of the 'weak tie' (friendly, superficial connections), they spread ideas far.
- **Mavens** – information specialists – are subtly different. They focus on the needs of others rather than their own, and have the most to say. Teachers are a good example.
- **Salespeople** concentrate on the relationship, not the message, and are persuasive because they have better 'sales' skills, non-verbal communication and 'motor mimicry' (imitating others' emotions and behaviour to gain trust).

Tipping points need connectors, mavens and salespeople.

2 The stickiness factor

With products or ideas, how attractive it is matters as much as how it is communicated in determining whether it spreads. Its 'stickiness' determines whether it passes by or catches on. To reach a tipping point, ideas have to be compelling and attractive. The Information Age has created a stickiness problem – the clutter of messages we face leads to products being ignored. To create epidemics, it is increasingly important to present the message effectively. If contagiousness is a function of the messenger, stickiness is a property of the message.

3 The power of context

We rarely appreciate how our personal lives are affected by circumstances. Changes in the context of a message can create an epidemic. An example is the 'broken windows theory' – if someone sees a single broken window, that person may believe there is an absence of control and authority. Consequently, they are more likely to commit other crimes. A broken window or graffiti invites more serious crimes, spawning a crime wave. Gladwell argues that our circumstances, or context, matter as much as character and that we can control the tipping point by altering the environment.

GRIP

Building customer motivation

Successful selling involves showing customers how your product will make a difference to them. Use GRIP to understand a client's goals, assess their situation, and identify the gap between what they have and what they would value and their motivation to buy.

The four stages are:

- Goals
- Reality
- Implications
- Plan.

Stage	Your aims	How	Result
Goals: building a vision Thinking about the future creates a positive mindset that sees opportunities, is motivated to change and ready to see how your offer will make a difference	Help the client see how their current situation could be improved Encourage them to question and challenge the present, think enthusiastically and creatively and build a vision of the future	Ask open questions about the future – encouraging customers to create a vision of the future and realize what's lacking While knowing their current situation, focus on the future	Everyone is clear about the gap between where they are and where they would like to be The client is thinking about possibilities and wanting to achieve their vision
Reality: what stands between you and your goals Explore the current situation in detail	Clarify what needs to be done to make the client's ideal solution happen	Ask questions about their current situation: what they like and what frustrates them	Client sees the extent of the gap and the need for action If no gap exists, time is saved not pursuing the sale further

Stage	Your aims	How	Result
Implications: seeing a different future Explore the implications and importance of change. Move the client towards a decision Don't rush to your offer because this stage provides valuable insight to better tailor your offer	Not to rush to making an offer Establish a good relationship with client Understand their needs and hopes	Be empathetic, listen and ask questions that explore the situation and goals Help client to see the extent of the gap and understand the difference change would make	Knowing client's commitment Developing trust and a strong relationship An enthusiastic client
Plan: achieving your goals Use the information to tailor your offer, build relationships and gain commitment	Enable your client to achieve goals, offering the solution for their needs Ensure customer feels unrushed, comfortable and confident Make the right sale – for repeat business	Use information so solution meets their needs and expectations Work with client to make adjustments	The sale A long-term business relationship

MANAGING INFORMATION, TECHNOLOGY AND OPERATIONS

THE INFORMATION LIFE CYCLE

Using information to its full effect

A modern competitive company is only as good as its ability to use information.

Overview

Improving how your organization gathers and uses information will enhance analysis, decision-making, operations and strategic development. This starts with knowing how information flows, what it is used for and how it is applied. This is known as the information life cycle. How you use information at every stage of this cycle is critical to achieving targets, optimizing performance and revealing new opportunities.

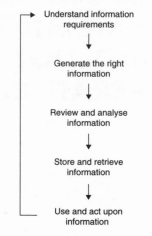

Start by understanding what information your company needs – and why it is needed

This will enable you to gather the right data for all aspects of your company and to put systems in place to ensure that it is routinely gathered, consistent, reliable and made available to yourself and others now and in the future. To do this, you will need to ask others what information they need (including the best sources of that data) and when they need it.

Then, generate the right data

Make sure that the information is fit for purpose. For the right decisions to be made, the right data has to be collected. There are two aspects to this: generating the data you know you will need and gathering data that has yet to reveal valuable insight. Too often, information remains hidden – to be of use, it must be gathered, collated and organized effectively.

Next, review and analyse the information

How you review and analyse the information will determine the quality of problem-solving, decision-making, operational management and strategic development. To review the current situation, make sense of data and to highlight trends, gaps, strengths, weaknesses and opportunities, subject the information to quantitative methods, rigorous assessment and discussions.

Make sure that you store the information and are able to retrieve it

To be effective and of use, information needs to be stored properly and it needs to be cost-effective. It needs to be widely available and easily accessible. Make sure that it is clearly labelled and organized – and that people know how to access it. Also, information should be kept relevant and up to date.

Finally, use and act upon the information

Surprisingly, given that gathering information is an expensive, time-consuming process, some people neglect to follow through fully on what the data is telling them. To be of use, you have to be prepared to listen to what the data is saying and be prepared to take action – choosing to ignore the data is likely to lead strategy in the wrong direction, fail to resolve a problem or leave opportunities untapped. By improving the quality of how you identify the information you need and how information is gathered, analysed and stored, you will be better able to see what needs to happen, to make the right decisions, and to guide strategy and implementation.

INFORMATION ORIENTATION

Understanding the connection between investments in IT and improvements in business performance

What is the connection between a company's investments in IT and improvements in bottom-line performance? The answer lies with its Information Orientation.

Developed by Professor Donald Marchand, Information Orientation provides a framework for building and managing strategic IT capabilities that will optimize their value to organizations. His approach encompasses three information capabilities:

1 Information behaviours and values
2 Information management
3 IT practices.

These capabilities work together and determine how effectively companies use information. The 15 competencies within these capabilities can be seen below in the Information Orientation Maturity model (*source*: Professor Donald Marchand):

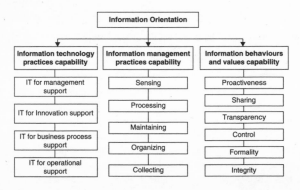

Information management practices

Enabling your organization to focus on the right information requires the correct processes to be established and managed and it needs employees to be properly trained to use them. This involves sensing, processing, maintaining, organizing and collecting information. Also, to improve the quality of information that is made available, it is essential to avoid (or minimize) information overload.

Information technology practices

Business strategy and IT strategy are inseparable. IT applications and infrastructure reach every aspect of running a business, from supporting operations and business processes to innovation and decision-making.

In their research, Donald Marchand and William Kettinger found that companies do not always have the same information capabilities in all their units. To be of most use and to avoid potentially damaging gaps, the Information Orientation measures need to be applied consistently throughout the organization.

Information behaviours and values

Organizations need to promote the information behaviours and values that are needed for the effective use of information – integrity, formality, control, transparency, sharing and proactiveness – and remove the barriers that impede information flow and use.

SIX SIGMA

The technique for measuring and improving product quality

Sigma is a term that is used to show how much something deviates from the norm (or target). Six Sigma uses statistical analysis and benchmarking to identify these deviations in order to improve quality and efficiency. Originally developed by Motorola to deal with manufacturing issues, it is now used in many other business contexts.

Six Sigma is a disciplined, data-led approach to measuring and evaluating costs. By measuring how much costs add value for customers, Six Sigma is useful for managing costs effectively and improving operations and strategy. By exposing costs that do not add value, companies can eliminate them and divert resources accordingly. Advantages include:

- improved performance and the elimination of waste
- efficient operations and greater control over quality issues
- reduced costs and increased profitability
- decisions and strategy informed by actual data
- focus on adding value for customers
- increased employee engagement and commitment
- setting targets, and focusing people on achieving them.

Using Six Sigma

Six Sigma involves identifying problems and non-value-adding costs and then improving processes and reducing waste as much as possible. The aim is to get a system to operate with Six Sigma quality – a state where defects are minimal. The process in question is measured against benchmarks 1–6 to judge efficiency, where level 6 is the best. For example, a manufacturing process that operates with only 3.4 defects per million outputs would equate to level 6.

A key aspect of the technique is to appoint senior people to champion Six Sigma and for them to create teams of experts to plan and execute the project. The process involves five main steps (known by the acronym DMAIC) with an optional sixth step (T):

1 **Defining the opportunity.** The project's exact purpose and parameters should be clearly stated and should factor in customer requirements.
2 **Measuring performance.** Relevant and revealing data should be collected.
3 **Analysing the opportunity.** Identify problems and where the causes lie.
4 **Improving performance.** Design new methods and test them through analysis, simulations or pilot tests.
5 **Controlling performance.** Set up procedures that continually monitor performance so that any problems can be immediately highlighted and dealt with.
6 **Transferring best practice.** Improvements, information and ideas should be spread throughout the company.

DMAIC is used to evaluate existing processes. A variation on this, known as DMADV (the last two letters standing for Design an alternative and Verify the new design), is used for projects aiming to create a new process.

KAIZEN

Ensuring continual improvement through gradual change

The Kaizen approach involves making small, gradual and continual improvements to business processes.

Overview

Popularized by Masaaki Imai, Kaizen sees quality improvements as a company-wide process, involving everyone, at every level. In particular, it emphasizes the role of people who use the processes because they are best placed to recognize where changes should be made – thereby tapping into a huge source of talent, knowledge and ideas. By using your existing workforce and making gradual changes, you are more likely to minimize expenditure on experts, capital costs and expensive research and development teams. By encouraging everyone to think about how to improve quality, you promote teamwork and foster people's pride in their work and their sense of shared ownership of the company's future – where people are motivated and all pulling in the same direction.

Succeeding with Kaizen

To adopt a Kaizen approach, do the following:

- Encourage, empower and enable the people who carry out an activity to suggest improvements.
- Aim to make many gradual and continual improvements rather than radical changes.
- Use hard evidence and quantitative methods to assess a situation.
- Consider creating Kaizen groups to meet regularly, to discuss issues and propose and develop improvements.

Kaizen certainly has its critics and it does have some problems and limitations:

- Its total approach can overshadow the potential contribution of key people and research and development teams. This can be addressed by managing talent – and each individual – appropriately and in the best way. For example, consider using the Nine-Box Grid (see No. 88).
- Kaizen's focus on everyday processes and its emphasis on gradual change is at odds with the current speed of innovation and market changes and the huge advantages that arise from leaps in thinking and approaches (particularly the concept of 'value innovation').
- Employees can feel undue pressure to be constantly thinking of how to improve. While, for some, the pressure to think how to improve is valuable, the key is to ensure that pressure does not become stress.

MANAGING KNOWLEDGE

Making the most of your organization's information, expertise and experience

Knowledge is a powerful company asset. Capturing, managing realizing and using knowledge in all its forms to create extra value and advantage is the lifeblood of successful organizations.

Overview

Knowledge in organizations often lies dormant because it is not recognized as having potential. Companies need to actively look for sources of knowledge and consider how best to use that information. A large stumbling block is the accessibility of information that resides in different parts of a company. IT overcomes this problem, linking parts of a company and making the information accessible to everyone. By centralizing information and encouraging people to use it, knowledge becomes a powerful company asset.

There are many sources of knowledge, including: your people, customers, intellectual property, databases, research and links with external experts. Customers should not be overlooked or underused – they are not constrained by internal thinking traps, may have ideas for products that are clearly sought after and form a ready-made target market.

Peter Drucker believes that the way in which companies manage knowledge determines their success. He divides the process into capturing knowledge, storing information, generating ideas and distributing information.

Capture	Generate ideas
Encourage everyone to pool and share their knowledge, to enable others to use it	Promote an innovative culture where everyone feels positive about suggesting new ideas
Store information	**Distribute information**
Develop the right IT system that is capable of storing and ordering information effectively as well as being easily accessible	Create an atmosphere where everyone shares information rather than holding it back to promote their own position

Effective knowledge management is not simply about amassing as much information as possible and storing it. The information needs to be ordered and stored efficiently, to enable the right people to access the right information easily and quickly. Information overload – not being able to see the wood for the trees – is no good to anyone. This is not to say that access should be limited – anyone should be able to access information, with the exception of anything sensitive. The point is that people should be aware of what information is likely to be relevant to them (and how to access it) and encouraged to use it and to share their own knowledge and information.

ACHIEVING A WIN–WIN OUTCOME

The six pitfalls of negotiations

By learning where the pitfalls lie in negotiations, it is possible to sidestep them and ensure results that last for all the parties involved.

Harvard Business School professor James Sebenius argues that six mistakes are responsible for the failure of negotiations. By avoiding them you can negotiate your way to success. These pitfalls are as follows:

1 **Neglecting the other side's problems.** If you do not understand the problems your negotiation partner needs to overcome, you will not offer them the correct solution and you will lose an effective bargaining chip.

2 **Letting price bulldoze other interests.** It is easy to focus exclusively on price. Make sure you consider other important factors – such as creating a positive working relationship and goodwill between both sides, and a deal-making process that is respectful and fair to everyone.

3 **Letting positions drive out interests.** While two sides of a debate may have opposing positions, they may also have compatible interests. Rather than working to persuade someone to abandon their position, it can be more productive to work on innovating and creating a deal that is able to satisfy a range of interests. Here, keep the big picture in mind: don't give up or fail because the detailed working is difficult or frustrating.

4 **Searching too hard for common ground.** Common ground can help negotiations, but different interests allow both sides to get something out of the deal. The key is to give and get: don't simply look for disappointing compromises.

5 **Neglecting BATNA.** BATNA stands for 'best alternative to a negotiated agreement' – that is, the options if the deal falls through. These may include approaching other companies or adjusting your business model. By fully analysing your prospects – and your partner's prospects – you can decide what to offer in the negotiation and when to offer it.

6 **Failing to correct for skewed vision.** Two types of bias can be present – role bias and partisan perception. *Role bias* (the confirming evidence trap) is the tendency to interpret information in self-serving ways,

overestimating your chances of success. *Partisan perception* (the over-confidence trap) is the propensity to glorify your own position while vilifying opponents. Overcome these biases by placing yourself in the position of your 'opponent'.

Actions of successful negotiators

As well as an ability to avoid pitfalls, great negotiators also have other qualities:

- They understand the other side's aims, perspectives and experience – essential to persuading them why they should agree.
- They also thoroughly research an individual or company before negotiations. They do not limit research to information relevant to the deal. Broadening the scope to the industry, goals and market conditions provides extra weight in negotiations.
- They are measured and avoid being overly aggressive. They may show firmness but remember that mutual understanding and rapport is essential.
- Above all, they seek a 'win–win' outcome by thoroughly exploring the full range of potential agreements that would allow both sides to benefit from the negotiation.

THE FOUR FACES OF MASS CUSTOMIZATION

Cost-effective ways to tailor your products

Mass customization uses mass production methods that are capable of providing customers with tailor-made products.

Overview

Technological changes have ushered in a new era of delivering custom-made products on a large scale. Customers are able to choose different features so that products can match their own needs. It is used across a range of industries, greatly increasing both customer appeal and market opportunities. Although how this is done will depend on the nature of the product, IT facilitates mass customization and streamlines the process.

Successful mass customization strikes the right balance between offering choice and the costs involved and ease of use for customers. It is no good providing so much choice that the costs are prohibitive or the customer is so overwhelmed that they are put off making a purchase. It is essential to find out what features matter most to customers, along with any operational limitations, in order to set workable and profitable limits on available options. These choices need to be reviewed regularly to take advantage of new technology and changing demand, as well as maintaining competitiveness. Also, it is important to streamline the process and change your existing methods to ensure that production and processes can cope seamlessly and efficiently with the many different products that need to be built for each customer.

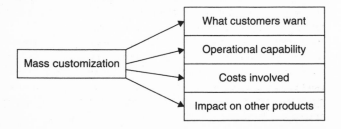

It is easy to get caught up in the whole process – with the potential of appealing to customers becoming the overriding focus and overlooking the significant logistical and financial problems involved. To be successful, the strategy must have a keen focus on capabilities, costs and the impact on your other products. As with all strategies, a company's overall profitability should be the priority.

Mass customization requires:

- a system for the customer to specify requirements easily (e.g. online ordering, call centre)
- advanced manufacturing systems that enable economies of scope, keeping cost and price low
- a build-to-order approach, with the product not made until the order is received
- a minimum-order quantity of one.

The four faces of mass customization

Writing in the *Harvard Business Review*, Joseph Pine and James Gilmore highlighted the four faces of mass customization:

1 **Collaborative customization.** The consumer and producer work together to define customer requirements. Examples include computers, clothing and footwear, furniture and some services.
2 **Adaptive customization.** The product is designed so that users can alter it themselves to fit unique requirements on different occasions. Examples include high-end office chairs and certain electronic devices.
3 **Cosmetic customization** (also called 'personalization'). The product is unique in appearance only. Examples include putting a customer's chosen text or image on T-shirts, mugs, pens and so on.
4 **Transparent customization.** The producer provides customized product without the consumer being necessarily being aware that it has been customized. This can be used when consumers' needs are predictable or can be easily deduced, and when customers do not want their requirements repeated. Examples include repeat orders for customized clothing or specialist chemicals.

PROCESS MANAGEMENT

Putting customers at the heart of your business processes

Process management cuts across departments and functions and seeks to group tasks together to improve the way they work and, importantly, to deliver greater value to customers.

Overview

Process management measures, monitors, analyses and improves business activities, making processes efficient, responsive and adaptable. Re-engineering, as Michael Hammer advocated, is imperative because, by focusing on process improvements, companies are better placed to enhance the value they provide to customers. Fundamentally, to get the most from process management it has to be part of the organization's culture. Looking for ways to improve should be part of people's thinking and approach, and change should be welcomed, not reluctantly accepted.

There are many different routes to managing and transforming processes. Accenture's Five Rs outline how to improve a process:

1 Reconfigure
2 Reorder
3 Reallocate
4 Relocate
5 Reduce

Accenture also highlights the qualities of process excellence. A process should:

- deliver the most value and get rid of waste
- be clearly outlined, with details of the process stored and accessible

- be easy to understand and follow and have flexibility
- minimize the time spent on it
- provide immediate feedback
- be linked to the company's other processes
- be focused on customers and be user-friendly.

TOTAL QUALITY MANAGEMENT (TQM)

Putting quality at the heart of your business

Total Quality Management is an all-encompassing approach to quality throughout an organization. It makes quality the business of everyone in the company and puts it at the heart of every business operation.

TQM seeks to raise standards, ensure minimum standards and make continual improvements for the benefit of customers and stakeholders. It is simply an approach. How it is achieved varies according to the preferences and priorities of each company, with the processes, tools and measurements employed supporting the principle itself.

TQM maintains quality and improves products and practices to deliver advantages that improve competitiveness, profitability and long-term success. As well as minimizing waste, it empowers and motivates individuals, promotes teambuilding, secures customer loyalty and improves relationships with suppliers. With processes measured against a standard, expected outcome, quality can be monitored effectively and efficiently – with shortfalls immediately highlighted. TQM reaches every part of a company, from corporate responsibility to organizational culture.

Key points
- **Everyone needs to be committed to delivering and improving quality standards.** Leaders need to be behind TQM and gain the commitment of everyone in the company – by empowering, motivating and encouraging positive participation.
- **Focus on goals and what is needed.** Be clear about your purpose, vision and what you want TQM to achieve. Focus on customer needs (current and future). Importantly, your goals need to be realistic and achievable.
- **Don't be distracted.** Being overly focused on securing certificates and awards blinkers thinking and misses potential. By focusing too much on

processes, TQM can cement suboptimal practices and anchoring traps. This is a failure of how TQM is implemented rather than the principle itself.

- **Market awareness.** TQM would be of limited use without market awareness (including possible changes in tastes or technology). Understanding what others are achieving (inside and outside your industry) will help you to remain competitive and identify opportunities.

- **Integrate TQM into all activities.** Put processes in place so that TQM runs smoothly, is easy to use, becomes an automatic part of operations and is transparent (employees should not feel spied on or undermined).

- **Manage the extra workload.** Manage the extra workload TQM places on employees by ensuring that your people have a positive attitude towards TQM and can incorporate changes without being demotivated. TQM should not distract employees from their main activities.

- **Use appropriate measures.** Measurements need to be accurate and revealing. Subject your approach to criticism by asking: Are you measuring the right things, and how can measures be improved?

- **Use the information.** Use data to inform decision-making and strategy and to achieve continual improvements and long-term growth. Analysis needs to be perceptive, insightful and creative. The information should be organized and stored so that it is easily accessible and of use to others.

- **Be prepared for the full impact.** TQM is a way of thinking that pervades the entire company. This affects every aspect of running a business – from employee motivation, refocusing priorities and changing business practices through to changes in culture and strategic direction.

THE EFQM MODEL

A practical guide to managing quality

The EQFM model is a quality-management tool that is used to assess how a company's systems and processes are performing, and also to inform strategy and business re-engineering.

Overview

Named for the European Foundation for Quality Management, the model aims to assess and inform the design of a company's structures, processes and management. At its core is the knowledge that quality management is not a fragmented, piecemeal activity: its reach is far broader. Quality and excellence are achieved by ensuring that all parts of a company work together effectively. Systems, procedures, strategy, resources and people all need to support one another and pull in the same direction.

How the EFQM model works

The model is highly customer-focused and results-driven and it shows how results can be achieved by exploring the links between what you are doing and the results you get. The model is divided into two main aspects: results and enablers, with results informing our learning to better inform enablers in the future.

- **Results** are reviewed over four areas: key performance, people, customers and society.
- **Enablers** are examined through five categories: leadership, people, policy and strategy, partnerships and resources, and processes.

Using the right performance indicators and monitoring techniques is critical – based on the philosophy that what gets measured gets managed. The information you gather is then used to set the right strategy, innovate and make further improvements. This builds an organization that learns, adapts and achieves more.

Learning and innovation

Successful companies learn from their results, and this learning feeds back into each of the five enablers. This cycle of assessing, measuring, learning and redesigning is a continuous process that reaches into all aspects of running a company, including softer issues such as culture, levels of employee engagement and leadership. Quality management is not simply concerned with technical processes; these are important but they are not the only factors we need to consider. Like any system, parts that work together build on each other constructively, amplifying the benefits. So it is with quality management: hard and soft issues need to be on the same page, supporting one other.

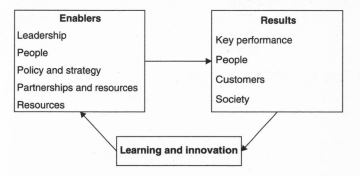

For each enabler, with reference to results, review how it is working and identify what works well, any gaps that exist, what needs to be done better and how all the enablers either work together or create barriers to achieving excellence.

THE DEMING CYCLE: PLAN – DO – CHECK – ACT

Planning for improvement

The Deming Cycle promotes learning and continuous improvement through its four sequential steps: Plan – Do – Check – Act.

The model provides a clear, logical process for making continuous improvements, and focuses your thinking on the actual details and on what your purpose and objectives are so that you can better turn your goals into reality. Importantly, it breaks companies out of the Plan – Do – Plan – Do approach by formally building measurement, review, amendments and learning into the process. The cycle is self-explanatory:

- **Plan** – draw up a plan
- **Do** – implement the plan
- **Check** – measure and assess progress
- **Act** – make necessary refinements

Critically, the experience, information, feedback and analysis you learn at each stage is then used to improve the current plan and subsequent projects.

The cycle of learning

Each step will obviously cover many factors, and these will differ from project to project and company to company, depending on the issues and circumstances faced.

Plan

Gather information about what is currently happening and think about what you would like to happen.

Decide:

- what you would like the future to look like
- what your goals are
- the impact on those involved – and their likely responses. How can these be handled effectively?
- how your goals can be achieved.

Draw up an implementation plan – know what is to be done, and when.

Do

Implement the plan carefully.

Make sure your people have the necessary training.

Changes are best introduced in discrete steps so that results can be accurately measured.

Act

Roll out the successful changes you've made to other functions.

Use the information, learning and experience from this experience both to plan further improvements to this plan and to inform new projects.

Check

Collate all measurements, feedback and information.

Assess how the plan is working.

Determine whether the goals have been achieved.

SUPPLY CHAINS

Adding value at every stage of your business

Supply chain management is about achieving success – not just for yourself but for others. No matter where your company is placed in the supply chain, it is important to understand the whole chain so that you can better manage and support everyone involved – that way, everyone wins.

Overview

Maximizing profits for your company is best achieved by understanding the needs of your suppliers and the companies you supply. This requires one basic component that is often neglected: strong business relationships in general and great communication in particular. By talking to your suppliers and clients you will better understand their needs and capabilities, but, more than that, you will be able to create a dialogue where you can all develop a better route to success. Figuring things out together is the core of supply chain excellence.

Business strategy needs to start by looking at how the supply chain is structured. Your approach will reflect the needs of your company. You also need to be creative. Are there new technologies that could rewrite your current supply chain? Could you cut out your current clients and sell direct to customers?

Example: supply chain for a car company

Raw materials e.g. mining company producing aluminium ore → Primary manufacturer e.g. company producing sheet aluminium → Fabricator e.g. company that turns aluminium sheets into car parts → Product producer e.g. company that assembles parts into cars → Consumer marketer e.g. the company or division that markets the car → Retail e.g. the local dealer that sells the car directly to customers

Upstream organizations   Downstream organizations

Centre of gravity

Each company is dependent on the others in the supply chain. This means that everyone needs to consider the needs of other companies and, most importantly, the ultimate end user: the customer. The advantages of cutting stages out of the supply chain are self-evident: better prices for customers, faster service and greater control, and competitive advantage. Essentially, supply chains require careful management: companies rely upon one another. By developing the right strategy together, everyone wins.

FINANCE, ACCOUNTING AND ECONOMICS

RATIO ANALYSIS

Revealing measurements

Ratios assess business performance at strategic and operational levels. When compared to ratios for previous periods, they show trends and patterns.

Use the most effective ratios for each situation and choose appropriate time periods. Knowing the ratios other organizations monitor provides access to similar information. Use ratios creatively and extensively to provide insight into performance. Make sure that everyone knows what the ratio measures and what it means – use graphs to reveal trends. A ratio measures only one aspect and is only as good as the data it is based on. Moreover, its value depends on interpretation. Understanding causes requires further analysis.

Gross profit margin ratio

This is the relationship between revenue and costs. If gross profit is too low, either prices are too low or costs are too high

Gross profit ÷ Sales x 100 = Gross profit margin

Net profit ratio

This is the relationship between revenue and costs. If it is too low, or falling, costs may be rising or revenue falling.

Net profit ÷ Sales x 100 = Net profit margin

Average debtor collection periods

365 x Debtors (amount owed to your business) = Average debtor collection period

Average creditor payment period

365 × Creditors (amount owed by your business) = Average creditor
payment period

Current ratio

This is normally between 1.5 and 2. If it is less than 1, current liabilities exceed current assets, thus risking insolvency (though thus depends on the industry).

Current assets ÷ Current liabilities = Current ratio

The quick ratio (acid test)

The quick ratio deducts from current assets those assets difficult to turn into cash quickly. This is normally between 0.7 and 1. If it stands at 1 or more, quick assets exceed current liabilities and the business is safe.

Quick assets ÷ Current liabilities = Quick (or 'Acid test') ratio

The gearing ratio

This measures solvency. Apart from new and small businesses, gearing should not exceed 50 per cent.

Loans + Bank overdraft ÷ Equity + Loans + Bank overdraft = Gearing

The price/earnings ratio (P/E)

This values a company.

Share price ÷ Earnings per share = Price/earnings ratio

The higher the P/E ratio, the more the company is worth. This is relative to competitors. Earnings rise when share prices rise – which can be misleading. Past earnings may not reflect future growth.

RATIO ANALYSIS

Return on equity

Net profit after tax ÷ Equity capital = Return on equity

Fluctuations in a supplier's prices

Supplier's current prices ÷ Supplier's previous prices

Suppliers' delivery times

Value of outstanding orders with suppliers ÷ Value of average
daily purchases

A supplier's reliability

Value of overdue orders from a supplier ÷ Average daily purchases
from all suppliers

Employee productivity

Profit ÷ Number of employees

Value-added per employee

Sales minus material costs ÷ Average number of employees

Sales growth

Sales for the period ÷ Sales for a previous period = Sales growth

Market share, to monitor product portfolio

Current market share ÷ Previous market share = Market share ratio

Value of work in hand

Value of orders in hand ÷ Average value of daily sales = Size of order book

Marketing efficiency

This is sales to cost ratio.

Marketing spend ÷ Revenue = Marketing efficiency

MAPPING AND MITIGATING RISK

Can you afford not to?

In order to minimize the chances of things going wrong, it is important to focus on the quality of what people do: doing the right things right reduces risks and costs.

Mapping risk

If the ability to control the risk is plotted against its potential impact, as shown in the diagram below, you can decide on actions either to exercise greater control or to mitigate the potential impact. Risks falling into the top-right quadrant are the priorities for action, although the bottom-right quadrant (total/significant control, major/critical impact) should not be ignored, as management complacency, mistakes and a lack of control can lead to the risk being realized.

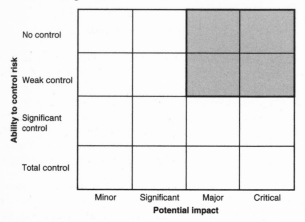

Quantifying potential risks

Because each risk may have a different level of impact, quantifying their effects is essential. Risks can be mapped both in terms of likely frequency and potential impact, with the emphasis on significance. Also, the potential consequences of risk may be ranked on a scale ranging from inconvenient to catastrophic.

When mitigating risks, start by reducing or eliminating those that result only in cost: essentially non-trading risks (these might include property damage risks, legal and contractual liabilities and business interruption risks, and can be thought of as the 'fixed costs' of risk). Other ways that risks can be reduced or mitigated are to share them with a partner, to monitor them or subject them to contingency plans. For example, acceptable service-level agreements from vendors are essential to reduce risk. Joint ventures, licensing and agency agreements are also different ways of mitigating risk.

Finally, actively managing and using information is also crucial. Risk management relies on accurate, timely information. Management information systems should provide details of the likely areas of risk and of the information that is needed to control the risks. This information must reach the right people at the right time, so that they can investigate and take corrective action.

SHAREHOLDER VALUE ANALYSIS

Consistently increasing the value of a business for shareholders

Shareholder value analysis sees the worth of a company as the long-term value it creates for shareholders. Originally proposed by Alfred Rappaport, it can be applied to the whole company, a business unit or specific project and is used to determine a company's direction and to measure progress.

Dealing with long-term profit forecasts, it focuses efforts on creating long-term shareholder value. Freeing strategic thinking from the limitations of other financial measures that can be overly focused on past data or short-term issues, it better informs a company's strategy and puts the focus on securing future financial stability and growth. This makes it particularly important for determining the long-term direction of a company or business unit. A significant advantage is that it can be used across a range of operating units, regardless of any differences between financial measures that are in place.

The method

Obviously, the calculations involved in shareholder value analysis are many and complex. The following is designed to show the general principle of what is being determined.

- First, estimate the total net worth of a company, unit or project – that is, *assets minus liabilities.* (This involves using discounted cash flows and subtracting expected capital costs.)
- Then divide this by the number (or value) of shares. This reveals the return to shareholders:

    (total net worth − liabilities) ÷ number of shares = return

- If this return is higher than the costs involved, then value has been created for shareholders – clearly, the larger this difference between return and costs (also known as equity return and equity costs), the more shareholder value is added.

return − costs = shareholder value

Limitations

Awareness of its limitations and being clear about what you expect to get out of the process will help you to use shareholder value analysis effectively.

- It involves painstaking assessment, valuation and analysis – these take considerable time and money.
- Predictions about future cash flows and costs can never be accurate. As well as basing the value of a company on guesses, these figures are subject to unforeseen changes.
- It can skew strategy to only considering shareholder value as a measure of worth. Not all value in a company lies in its return to shareholders. It is important not to lose sight of other factors, with different measures – such as corporate social responsibility, customers and employees.

SIX LEVELS OF STRATEGIC AGILITY AND COST CONTROL

Managing costs and preparing for the future

The future arrives quickly and in ways that continually surprise: only those ready to adapt will survive and prosper. Companies need to create processes that enable them to adapt easily, quickly and effectively to changes and opportunities without harming other parts of the company.

A company's processes do not exist separately from the people who run them. Administrators enable the rapid adaptation needed to succeed while protecting the whole company. By creating self-adaptive systems, companies are more than robust – they maximize potential. This requires redesigning systems to:

1 **enable** people to determine and make necessary changes so that processes adapt quickly, successfully and effectively
2 **decouple** processes so that changes in one part do not harm other parts.

The dangers of cost-cutting

When times are tough, companies cater to the short term and cut costs. However, long-term needs are important. John Wells has identified six typical responses from companies that are facing cost-cutting pressures:

- **Level Zero.** Leaders promise cuts but don't deliver – long-term success doesn't materialize. Their focus is on other, narrow goals – not on creating a company capable of rapid and successful adaptation.
- **Level One.** Drastic, arbitrary, ill-conceived cuts are made that fail to deal with the causes of difficulties. Only by resolving fundamental, structural causes can a company hope to redress the situation.
- **Level Two.** Redesigning processes to meet current needs. While this cuts immediate costs, it fails to build for the future. This leads to higher costs as the company repeatedly overhauls the system to keep pace with competitors.

- **Level Three.** Although future needs are considered, plans are constrained by the need to stagger initiatives according to what can be afforded.
- **Level Four.** Leaders plan for the unknown by creating adaptable systems that are decoupled from each other so that targeted changes can be made easily, without harming other activities.
- **Level Five.** Leaders ensure that companies can weather storms. Systems are decoupled and people are seen as enablers of those systems. Decoupling is the first step, but the right culture needs to be in place to make it happen. Trust and enable your people to assess situations and make changes quickly and effectively. This is when companies are agile and adaptive.

The problem of IT

IT structure is problematic: it is company-wide and an entrenched monolith – so much so that IT is often quoted as a major *barrier* to change. It is essential that IT does not impede the ability of individual parts of a company to adapt. Decoupling processes are necessary for adaptive systems.

Only by creating a culture of self-adaptation will companies be future-proof.

DISCOUNTED CASH-FLOW ANALYSIS

Understanding the time value of money

We all know that cars depreciate in value from the moment we drive away from the sales forecourt, and that the money cannot be spent on anything else. Essentially, discounted cash flow is no different. Money has a value – one that changes through time. Inflation means that cash today is worth more than cash tomorrow. That is where discounted cash flow comes in: it is a means of tracking true worth and guiding business and investment decisions.

Overview

When deciding where to invest, you need to take three things into account.

1 Is the risk worth the investment?
2 Are there other projects that would be more lucrative? That is, what is the opportunity cost of using the money in this way rather than on something else?
3 Will the return, over the estimated timescale, outdo inflation? In other words, would you have been better off investing your money elsewhere?

As a starting point, look at the current inflation rate, historical inflation rates, and possible future rates for the markets you are operating in. For example, if inflation is running at 2 per cent (and this is indicative of the historic trend and is unlikely to be eroded by future changes), you will know that, if you invest a certain sum over a certain period, you will need to obtain a return of at least the original sum plus this inflation figure – otherwise, you would have been better off spending your money elsewhere.

The five steps of discounted cash-flow analysis

These five steps will help you to determine the level of investment a project can justify.

1 Identify exactly how the investment will be used – including the timing of all costs and likely sales.
2 Determine both the positive and negative cash flows over time.
3 Estimate the cash flow for when the project has been fully implemented and is likely, given unchanging markets, to continue.
4 Apply the discounted cash-flow figure. This will reveal whether the original investment is worth making. This involves considering how much risk is involved, the cost of any loans, and inflation. This is not an exact science, so it is useful to create best-, medium- and worst-case scenarios. You will also need to consider the expectations of investors.
5 Finally, compare your discounted cash flow with each year of operations. Decide whether the returns justify the investment.

Importantly, profit is not simply a case of deducting costs from sales: it is about knowing the opportunity cost of your money.

ECONOMIES OF SCALE

Increasing your profit margins

High costs hit profits, and one vital way of reducing costs is to develop economies of scale where the cost of producing individual units falls as the volume of production increases.

Overview

Given that fixed costs need to be divided between the total number of units produced, the more units produced the lower unit costs become. Economies of scale can be achieved when your suppliers are able to offer lower prices for large orders, or because your own means of production reaches a large enough scale for goods to be produced more cheaply – perhaps through more efficient equipment or where fixed costs are divided over many more units.

The graph below shows the average cost per unit falling as production levels increase:

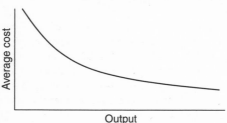

The benefits

Economies of scale:

- improve efficiency
- boost profitability
- may lead to price reductions

- enable resources to be used efficiently
- optimize output
- emphasize a focus on costs
- enable us to question current methods and look for improvements.

Why it matters

Achieving economies of scale is not simply about increasing profit margins. It is also about passing these savings on to customers by offering competitive prices, and benefiting shareholders and people who invest and risk their capital by building the value of the business.

Economies of scale are all about crunching the numbers and looking for ways to reduce those numbers even further. It may involve making substantial investments in new equipment. Again, it is a simple case of doing the sums: calculating all the costs, investment, price and expected sales and then seeing what comes out. The goal is to reduce *average unit costs* while being mindful of other considerations, such as the need to maintain an acceptable standard of quality and brand values.

The importance of managers taking economies of scale into account is clearly seen in the publishing industry. A short print run of a book is very expensive. The high fixed costs of the set-up are divided between a small number of books. These costs can be recouped only by charging a high price per book, which then has the disadvantage of being uncompetitively priced. When those high initial costs are spread over a larger print run, average cost per unit falls dramatically.

Admittedly, however, economies of scale are not always the only consideration – risk is also an important factor. Not only is there no point in achieving economies of scale if the product doesn't sell, it has simply exposed you to greater risk or limited your strategic options by tying money up. Nonetheless, economies of scale enable companies to be more competitive and to increase their profit margins.

PRICE ELASTICITY

The way things are priced

Elasticity determines how flexible prices are. If a product is highly elastic, a company will find it difficult to increase the price because customers can go elsewhere, either to competitors or to purchasing entirely different goods. If it is inelastic, sales are less dependent on price – perhaps there are few suppliers and the product is essential.

Can you charge more for a product? Price elasticity answers that simple question, indicating the price you can set, which markets to enter and the levels of justifiable investment.

- **If your product is highly sensitive to price changes,** focus on reducing costs or achieving market dominance by creating a stronger brand. Aim to create artificial scarcity or desirability to lower the price elasticity for your product. Alternatively, focus on reducing costs to raise profit margins.
- **If your product is less sensitive to price,** you can increase profit through higher prices because people have fewer options. With cost reductions, price inelasticity is a recipe for supra-normal profits. Theoretically – brand issues and company longevity aside – the ultimate goal in a free market is monopolistic profits. Here, high price inelasticity is ideal – enter quickly, scoop profits and switch lanes when others enter the market.

Because free markets are free, companies can never be certain about how secure their positions are. Companies that once enjoyed price inelasticity and now rest on their laurels may often find themselves on the wrong side of enterprising, innovative, disruptive start-ups with new technologies and better products. Also, when price inelasticity becomes too high for an essential product provided through few companies (an oligopoly), governments often step in and regulate prices.

Veblen goods

Usually, when prices rise, demand falls. However, with 'Veblen goods' (goods with snob value), demand rises when price increases. Here, perception is everything: customers value products *because* they are expensive.

Price elasticity in detail

Elasticity is calculated as the percentage change in demand divided by the percentage change in price. The negative or positive sign in the answer only indicates the relationship between demand and price. Except in the case of Veblen goods, the sign is usually negative because price rises reduce demand, so the negative sign is usually ignored. It is the *extent* of the change that indicates price elasticity:

- If the percentage change in demand is *less* than the change in price, demand is relatively inelastic. (See graph 1; the answer is less than one.)
- If the percentage change in demand is *greater* than the change in price, demand is relatively elastic. (See graph 2; the answer is greater than one.)

Graph 1   **Graph 2**

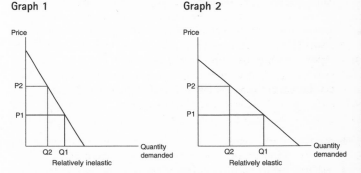

The area of the rectangle under each price/quantity combination reveals the impact of price levels on revenue.

SEVEN STEPS FOR SURVIVING A DOWNTURN

How businesses come through tough times stronger than before

What are the practical steps a business should take when faced with intensifying competition or a market downturn? There is no magic formula, just seven areas where practical action will help ensure continued success.

1 Develop the right strategy

A strategy has three elements: development, implementation and selling (gaining commitment and buy-in). Underpinning all three is choice, in particular the need to choose a distinctive, competitive position with three dimensions. These dimensions are:

1   who to target as customers (and who to avoid targeting)
2   what products to offer
3   how to undertake related activities.

2 Focus decisions on the most profitable areas

Concentrating on products and services with the best margin will protect or enhance profitability. This might involve redirecting sales and advertising activities.

3 Strengthen customer focus

Customer focus matters because this is how firms retain existing customers, sell more to existing customers and attract new business (from the market and also from competitors). This means segmenting markets and using data mining and the Internet for decision-making.

4 Increase sales revenue

This can be achieved by increasing the effectiveness of your pricing, sales teams, sales process, sales activities and channels – or a combination of all five. An invaluable technique here is measurement.

5 Manage the money

The financial issues that influence success are cash management, costs, revenue and investment. Keep control of costs, reduce them aggressively wherever possible, and manage your cash by controlling suppliers' and customers' payment terms.

6 Develop profitable new products

While it may be risky to develop a new product in a downturn, inaction may be riskier – the momentum of innovation is what will carry you beyond the downturn. If you stay the same during a period of increased competition and falling demand, you will fall even further and faster behind your competitors.

7 Remember the basics of sales, finance and leadership

- Match customers' needs and wants with your product.
- Meet with customers, gain their trust – and sell.
- Choose the best pricing strategy and consider using price innovations.
- Review past sales techniques and refine your approach.
- Make your product easy to buy.
- Develop an awareness of competitors and build your competitive advantage.
- Evaluate and develop the performance of sales teams.
- Review costs and understand cost structures.
- Manage debtors, purchasing, overheads and creditors.
- Demonstrate a desire to learn, not blame.
- Encourage people to find cost savings.
- Keep people informed.

Above all, keep your head. There is no silver bullet to surviving a downturn. It is a time for sound common sense, energy and calmness, and the business basics.

PERSONAL EFFECTIVENESS AND CAREER SUCCESS

THE SEVEN HABITS OF HIGHLY EFFECTIVE PEOPLE

How effective are you?

In his book *The Seven Habits of Highly Effective People*, writer Stephen Covey outlines the following set of activities and attitudes that promotes good leadership skills.

1 Be proactive

This involves self-determination and the power to decide the best response to a situation, so you can control your environment rather than it controlling you.

2 Begin with the end in mind

This is essential to both personal leadership and to leading others. To achieve your aims, concentrate on activities that are relevant. This will help you to keep focused, to avoid distractions and to be more productive and successful.

3 Put first things first

Effective personal management involves organizing and implementing activities that will help you and your team to achieve your aims. While habit 2 requires mental creation, habit 3 is about physical creation.

4 Think win–win

Leadership requires good interpersonal skills, as achievements often depend on the co-operation of others. Covey argues that win–win is based on two assumptions: there is plenty for everyone and success tends to follow a co-operative approach rather than the confrontation of win-or-lose.

5 Seek to understand first and then seek to be understood

Covey argues that for good communication you need to 'diagnose before you prescribe' – this is an extremely powerful tool.

6 Synergize

Leaders need to understand how to use co-operation creatively. Given the principle of the whole being greater than the sum of the parts, organizing co-operative activities to utilize each person's strengths will promote a successful outcome. Covey argues that this requires us to see both the good and the potential in the other person's contribution.

7 Sharpen the saw

Self-renewal both enables and strengthens the other habits. Covey divides the self into four parts – spiritual, mental, physical and social/emotional – which should all be developed if you wish to become a highly effective leader.

EMOTIONAL INTELLIGENCE

Using emotional intelligence to increase influence, fulfilment and success

Emotional intelligence (EI) is taking information from your own emotions and the emotions of others and then applying that knowledge in order to be more successful.

One of its key strengths is enabling us to sense and use emotions in order to manage situations better, improve decision-making and achieve positive outcomes. By recognizing, understanding and dealing with both our own emotions and those of others, we are more likely to be successful.

Developing emotional intelligence

We are all subject to emotions pulling us in directions that may or not be the best course of action. EI seeks to improve how we respond to emotions to get the most out of ourselves and others.

In *Emotional Intelligence: Why it can matter more than IQ*, psychologist Daniel Goleman details five emotional competencies. These are essential to managing ourselves and to leading people successfully:

1 Knowing your emotions – self-awareness
2 Managing emotions
3 Motivating yourself and others
4 Recognizing emotions in others and showing empathy
5 Handling relationships and staying connected.

The competency hierarchy

These emotional competencies are labelled 1–5 because they build on one another in a hierarchy. For example, we need to be able to identify our own emotional state (competency 1) if we are to manage our emotions (competency 2). Similarly, we need to achieve the first three competencies if we are to use empathy (competency 4) to influence others positively. Finally, the first four competencies are needed to maintain good, successful and productive relationships (competency 5). Each of these emotional competencies are described below.

1 Knowing your emotions – self-awareness

Previous emotional experiences influence our decision-making so it is important to be aware of all our emotions if we are to avoid any negative cycles and, instead, make better decisions.

2 Managing emotions

Once we can recognize these emotions, we can use this knowledge and develop strategies and responses to manage our emotions. This is true of the three main triggers to potentially negative outcomes: anger, anxiety and sadness. This is why EI is important during times of change.

3 Motivating yourself and others

It is not enough to know that you should create a supportive, enthusiastic environment; you have to know *how* to. In order to motivate others, we must understand individuals properly and use this information to achieve our aims. This involves being sensitive to what affects a person's enthusiasm and then providing the right approach.

4 Recognizing emotions in others and showing empathy

To influence others and gain their trust and commitment, it is essential to understand a person's emotions and then respond appropriately.

5 Handling relationships and staying connected

Whenever we relate to someone, there is an emotional transaction that passes between individuals. These interactions have an effect: they make us feel better or worse. This creates a secret economy that is the key to motivating people – a key that we can use to develop better relationships.

HEAD, HEART AND GUTS

An integrated approach to leadership

Head, hearts and guts is a shorthand way of saying that leaders and managers need to use three different styles of leadership if they are to be successful.

Overview

To succeed across a range of responsibilities – from making decisions and setting strategy to handling relationships, motivating others and resolving problems – leaders need to use different styles and approaches that are appropriate to each situation and the people involved, to ensure that a company's full potential is realized.

The success of each decision we make and implement depends on accessing a wide range of skills. For example, a strategy based on sound analytics will be ineffective without the courage, emotional intelligence and people skills that are also needed to make it happen.

Often, individuals rely on one preferred way of working, which leads to oversights, missed opportunities and underperformance. For example, relying predominantly on data and rational analysis (head) can make a leader too narrowly focused, while over-emphasizing emotional aspects (heart) can lead to flawed, ill-conceived strategy. Similarly, an almost exclusive dependence on courage (guts) to direct decisions and operations is likely to underestimate some key factors and the opinions of others.

Resolving the challenges leaders face requires brains, emotional intelligence and courage. Ensuring that leaders develop all three enables them to deploy the right approach at the right time to optimize an outcome and to ensure that decisions and relationships are not skewed by an over-reliance on one style. The holistic, integrated approach of head, heart and guts is effective because it sees situations from many angles, giving a fuller picture and a more appropriate way forward.

In practice: a systemic, integrated approach

David L. Dotlich, Peter C. Cairo and Stephen H. Rhinesmith advocate the holistic approach of head, heart and guts to avoid the damaging effects of leaders relying heavily on one method – such as not achieving performance improvements by failing to connect properly with others – and to enable leaders to deal with challenges and uncertainty and to operate effectively.

Implementing a four-stage process will help develop and empower leaders to use their brains, emotional intelligence and courage to meet the many challenges they face.

The four-stage process to developing an integrated approach

1	**Address systemic issues**
	Remove potential obstacles that inhibit the ability to show heart and guts behaviours or to challenge existing norms – such as a risk-averse culture.
2	**Involve the executive committee**
	Get everyone in the organization to buy into this new, integrated approach – it has to become part of the company's culture. For this to happen, you will need to secure the commitment of top management.
3	**Use leadership development as a diagnostic tool**
	Bring systemic issues to the attention of top management by encouraging those developing their leadership skills to provide feedback and to share their opinions.
4	**Customize the development programme**
	Ensure that the head, heart and guts approach is tailored to your company's specific needs and culture to enable it to be successfully integrated and of maximum benefit.

CAREER DEVELOPMENT PLANNING

Turbo-charge your career and help plan for future progression and success

Career planning needs careful consideration and it may help to create a personal profile highlighting relevant skills, experience, strengths and weaknesses. These can be matched with aspirations and likely challenges – both now and in the future.

Overview

Career and personal development planning enables people to move from where they are to where they want to be. Career planning is a lifelong process of nurturing, shaping and improving skills, knowledge and expertise, in order to enhance effectiveness and adaptability. Career planning also reduces the likelihood that skills will become out of date or obsolete.

It does not necessarily mean preparing for promotion or advancement, although that might be relevant from time to time. It is much more about improving and being ready for new challenges and changing circumstances. Development planning requires a personal commitment to develop and improve. In particular, this means understanding and accepting constructive criticism, and being willing to take measures to improve performance.

Develop your personal profile

This can be created by considering the following:

- **Priorities.** What values really matter to you personally? Do you know what sort of leader you want to be? It can also help to reflect back over your career and recollect leaders that you feel were particularly good or especially poor. Why did they succeed or fail?
- **Work experience.** What positions have you held? When did you succeed, and why? How could your performance have been better?

- **Achievements.** What have been your greatest achievements? What gave you greatest pleasure and what impressed others?
- **Personal attitudes.** Assessing how you behave in different situations can help to understand the way you feel and behave: where you are likely to be strong and when you might feel less certain. For example:
  - Are you energized around people or do you prefer to spend time alone?
  - Do you think quickly or do you tend to take time to reflect first?
  - Do you prefer to do a few things well or pursue many things superficially?
  - Are you an open person or more private?
  - Do you prefer order and structure or do you tend to live spontaneously, remaining open to possibilities?

Assess your future options and plans

The value of a personal profile lies in helping to understand yourself: what you like and dislike; where you succeed and fail; and where you are strong and weak.

There are several key questions that can help support an individual's career planning and development:

- What are your goals and aspirations? Why are these important?
- What is your timescale for achieving these goals, and what are the key milestones that will need to be achieved?
- Are your development plans in line with the goals you want to pursue?
- What opportunities are available – now and in the foreseeable future?
- How do your skills match with the business strategy?
- What further support do you need?
- How will you ensure success?

THE SELF-DEVELOPMENT CYCLE

Learning to build your skills and effectiveness

The self-development cycle is a method of planning development activities in a rigorous, thorough and practical way.

The success of the self-development cycle depends on repeating the planning process regularly (at least every year, preferably every six months or when circumstances change, such as taking on a new role). The seven stages of the cycle are:

1 Establish the purpose

You need to keep the overall aim firmly in mind and then ensure that all activities directly support this aim. Without this clear goal in mind it is often difficult to stay on track, keep momentum or maintain motivation.

2 Identify development needs

Identify development needs so that a programme for meeting those needs can be devised. In particular, the needs must be realistic and time-constrained, with a definite deadline.

3 Look at (and for) your opportunities for development

Deciding how to meet your development needs is the next stage and this may include a mix of formal and informal methods. As well as effectiveness, cost and timing, bear in mind your own preferred learning style: what approach suits you best?

4 Formulate an action plan

This will be necessary for more complex development needs requiring a range of activities or an ongoing process. You should also consider how the development process will be supported, perhaps by a mentor.

5 Complete the development activity

This is the core of the process. It is worth considering specifically how the results will be integrated into workplace activities.

6 Record outcomes

Keep track of development activities in order to assess results against planned objectives – reviewing progress and understanding what methods work best – and plan future activities.

7 Review and evaluate

Evaluating an event will help you assess whether the original objective has been met and the development need fulfilled.

PROBLEM-SOLVING TECHNIQUES

Finding the best solution

Resolving problems requires a logical and systematic approach to define the problem, generate solutions, and implement the best option.

Techniques to identify and understand the problem

Being thorough, critical and aware of hidden problem-solving traps, discussing issues and options with others, allowing time to reflect and testing and perfecting solutions will enable you to find the right course of action. Consider your personal style because, no matter how logical a solution seems, your emotions and values will affect your ability to follow through.

Cause-and-effect analysis

This deepens your understanding of the problem, identifying the root causes by collecting data and seeking the opinions of those involved.

Pareto analysis

Based on the view that 80 per cent of problems are caused by 20 per cent of possible causes, this analysis works best when there are only a few main causes that can be ranked. It does not work well for a large number of equally responsible factors. By ranking the causes, the most significant factors are revealed and the problem can be eliminated or its impact reduced.

Here are the four steps in Pareto analysis:

1 Identify the overarching problem.
2 Determine the causal factors and how often they occur.
3 List the biggest factors.
4 Develop a solution, targeting each factor individually.

Kepner-Tregoe (KT) analysis

This is particularly useful for the 'hard' management issues. Its methodical approach identifies what the problem is and explores the differences between what happens and what should happen by listing the possible causes of each problem or, where factors are linked, the whole problem. The process starts by asking:

- **What** is the problem or deviation?
- **Where** does it occur?
- **When** does it (or did it) occur?
- **How** does it occur – and how often?
- **How big** is the problem?

Techniques to generate options and solutions

- **When time is short:**
  - go ahead and try – if it doesn't work, try something else
  - do some test marketing
  - develop varied and diverse teams
  - get external input
  - reduce hierarchy
  - involve others – remove barriers to creative thinking
  - be less critical of failure – emphasize the importance of trying
  - impose deadlines, to focus efforts.
- **Heuristics** uses experience to guide decisions.
- **Mind-mapping** organizes thoughts and ideas clearly, to identify patterns and reveal new approaches.
- **Lateral thinking** combines ideas and concepts that haven't previously been brought together – think outside the box.
- **Question and challenge the way options are generated.** Provide a supportive environment that challenges traditional thinking.
- **Brainstorming** generates, discusses, develops and prioritizes options. When brainstorming, develop lots of ideas, suspend judgement, encourage free thinking, and cross-fertilize ideas.
- **Make and implement the decision.**
- **Select the most promising solution** and plan its implementation, and:
  - avoid procrastination, decision avoidance and over-analysis
  - manage risk – assess weaknesses and deal with them
  - value your intuition and experience
  - be confident in your decision and committed to achieving a solution.

THINKING FLAWS AND PITFALLS

It's not what we know that matters, but how we react to what we don't know

The way people think, as individuals and collectively, affects the decisions they make in ways that are far from obvious and rarely understood. John Hammond, Ralph Keeney and Howard Raiffa provide intriguing insights in this area.

Thinking flaws cause problems. Evaluate your vulnerability and find ways to counter each trap.

The traps of thinking flaws

- **The anchoring trap** leads us to give disproportionate weight to the first information that we receive. *Solution:* be sure about what is happening and ensure that you have all the information.
- **The status quo trap** biases us towards maintaining the current situation – even when better alternatives exist (caused by inertia or potential loss of face). *Solutions:* be open, honest and courageous.
- **The sunk-cost trap** inclines us to perpetuate past mistakes – 'we have invested so much in this we cannot alter course'. *Solution:* if it's spent, it's spent – worry about the present and future, not the past.
- **The confirming-evidence trap** results in seeking information to support the current situation and to ignore opposing information. *Solution:* avoid!
- **The framing trap,** when we incorrectly state a problem, undermines the decision-making process. *Solution:* see issues for what they are.
- **The over-confidence trap** makes us overestimate the accuracy of our forecasts. *Solution:* be self-critical.
- **The prudence trap** leads us to be over-cautious when estimating uncertain factors. *Solution:* be realistic.
- **The recent-event trap** leads us to give undue weight to recent or dramatic events. *Solution:* be aware of the trap and counter the danger it poses.

Fragmentation and groupthink

As well as thinking flaws, there are two pitfalls of organizational culture – fragmentation and groupthink:

- **Fragmentation** – people disagree, either with peers or superiors.
- **Groupthink** – people suppress ideas and support the group.

Overcoming thinking flaws

- **Be bold and don't fear consequences** – we over-estimate consequences and tend to discount our ability to make the right choice because of 'loss aversion', where we fear loss hurts more than gain.
- **Trust instincts and emotions** – we have evolved to make good decisions and manage their implementation.
- **Play devil's advocate** – searching for flaws and failings strengthens decisions and illuminates factors and biases affecting decisions.
- **Avoid irrelevancies** – be ready to question the information and its context.
- **Reframe the decision** – view issues from new perspectives.
- **Don't let the past hold you back** – regardless of past investments, look for better alternatives.
- **Challenge groupthink** – people are often afraid to comment because of social pressure. Find out what people really think.
- **Limit your options** – the more options we have, the harder decisions are. Ruthlessly cut through the options and choose the most promising.

FORCE FIELD ANALYSIS

Which way to go?

Developed by Kurt Lewin, Force Field analysis is a technique that identifies and reviews the conflicting factors affecting an either/or situation or decision in order to assess which of the two options is the correct route to take. It clarifies the issues involved, to help you make the right decision.

Overview

Force Field analysis can be applied to a wide range of issues and is particularly useful when our thinking over an issue has become stuck and we are unsure how to move forward. It works best for decisions or situations with two options. As it looks at the forces driving or blocking movement towards a goal, it is commonly used in coaching.

How it works

1 Create two tables side by side and write the decision that has to be made between them.
2 List the reasons (forces) for change in one table and the forces against change in the other. This list should be thorough and it should accurately and honestly reflect the thoughts, feelings and concerns of the person completing the analysis.
3 Assign a score to each force (1 being rated low, 10 being highly significant). Using weighted arrows is a good way to depict the relative significance of each force. Consider the score you assign to each factor.
4 Total the scores for each side.
5 Review the result:
   a Determine whether the list was as comprehensive and accurate as it could be and reflect on why each force was included and why some factors were left out.
   b Consider why you assigned a particular score to each factor.
   c Decide what the different totals mean to you and how they will influence the decision you make.

6 Reach a decision and examine your goals. As well as seeing the larger picture and weighing up the relative merits of each option, you can then examine the forces in more detail in order to determine the best way to implement your decision – such as whether to change career. Also, while Force Field analysis is used to explore a current choice that has to be made, it can act as a springboard to considering your goals in more detail.

Example of Force Field analysis used to consider a career change

Forces for change	Score			Forces against change	Score
More money	8	→	←	Sunk cost – already started current career	2
Better work–life balance	7	→	←	Effort required to find the right job	3
Better long-term prospects	5	**CHANGE** → ← **CAREER**		Competitiveness of the job market	3
More stimulating and varied	4	→	←	Lack of relevant experience	5
Greater responsibility	6	→	←	Concerns about self-confidence	7
Greater emphasis on developing new skills	2	→	←	Fear of failure	7
Total	**32**			**Total**	**27**

DEVELOPING PEOPLE, ORGANIZATIONS AND CULTURE

THE NINE-BOX GRID

Assessing performance and potential

The Nine-Box Grid measures individuals' performance and potential – identifying areas for improvement and highlighting their development needs.

Overview

The Nine-Box Grid is especially popular in organizations and among professionals who are particularly focused on developing their current and potential leaders, and for whom developing talent is a priority. In essence, it takes a view of an individual's success and effectiveness in their current role (performance), while adding the perspective of their future potential – what they are capable of contributing and achieving. The grid can help organizations understand what is needed for success both now and in the future, and how to ensure that people are recruited and developed in the most effective way possible, benefiting the organization and each individual.

The grid's greatest value lies in the dialogue it creates and the focus it provides. The multiple perspectives provide for a much more accurate assessment than simply one person's opinion. Also, the process helps to identify development needs as well as highlighting where performance needs to be improved.

Using the Nine-Box Grid: key questions

When assessing a person's performance and potential, it can help to keep several questions in mind:

- How well have they achieved their goals and objectives? What evidence is there?
- What do they do successfully and how can they improve their performance?
- What are this person's motivations? How can I get them engaged with the changes that are needed?

- What are their development needs? What activities might work best to help them make progress and achieve their potential?
- What will success look like?

	Trusted professional	Strong performer	Top talent
High/above target (approximately 15% of an organization's employees)	*High performance, low potential* • high performer, may be hard to replace (e.g. specialist role) • may be a technical expert – focus on retention and motivation • reached career potential – provide support, perhaps encourage them	*High performance, medium potential* • Significantly exceeds expectations and has potential (and possibly expects) to be promoted • Find ways to develop their potential e.g. coaching, stretch goals or new assignments	*High performance, high potential* • Has clear capacity to advance beyond their current role • Significantly exceeds objectives – may push boundaries and press for change
	Skilled	**Core performer with potential**	**Strong potential**
Medium/on target (approximately 75%)	*Performance meets expectations, low potential* • Solid performer, possibly a specialist, but with limited potential for promotion • Consider coaching from manager	*Performance meets expectations, medium potential* • Delivers expectations and has the potential to do more • Needs to be developed, tested and challenged – find ways to stretch and test their abilities	*Performance meets expectations, high potential* • Under-utilized talent who could achieve even more • Find ways to stretch, stimulate and develop (or they may leave)
	Watchlist	**Weak performer**	**Emerging Star**
Low/below target (approximately 10%)	*Low/unacceptable performance, low potential* • Performance is weak and unacceptable and potential may have been reached • Find ways to improve performance – consider development activities, a move to another role, or exit	*Low/unacceptable performance, medium potential* • Good potential but underperforms against objectives • Focus on their motivation and fit with the role. They may be in the wrong role, consider redeployment	*Low/unacceptable performance, high potential* • May be new to the role • Strong potential but may need support to improve performance • Manage closely, set SMART objectives and help them succeed
	Low/limited	Medium/can be developed	High/new challenge needed

(Vertical axis: Performance. Horizontal axis: Potential)

The aspiration for most organizations is to have their employees in the shaded areas of the grid; here, they are either performing to the best of their ability, or they are strong performers with the ability to go even further.

By using the opinions of several people, the Nine-Box Grid generates more accurate assessments. The process also helps to focus thinking on what exactly is expected of leaders and what success looks like.

THE MYERS-BRIGGS TYPE INDICATOR

Using personality types

The Myers-Briggs Type Indicator (MBTI) assessment is a psychometric test to identify personality types and to understand how people perceive the world and make decisions. These types reveal an individual's preferred way of thinking that affects how they view themselves, relate to others and approach situations, problem-solving and decision-making.

MBTI is based on Carl Jung's psychological types, and organizes types into four opposite *pairs* of personality preferences in four categories (Attitudes, Perceiving Functions, Judging Functions and Lifestyle):

1	Attitudes:	**Extraversion**	or **Introversion**
2	Perceiving Function:	**Sensing**	or **Intuition**
3	Judging Function:	**Thinking**	or **Feeling**
4	Lifestyle:	**Judging**	or **Perceiving**

These pairs are assigned letters to highlight which combination is dominant – there are 16 combinations. MBTI does not assess ability or make value judgements. It simply identifies the main personality type – for example, while people can use all four Perceiving and Judging Functions (sensing, intuition, thinking and feeling) at different times, they tend to use one more than the others. The combinations are revealing. For example, the four Functions operate in conjunction with the Attitudes, with each Function being used in either an extraverted or introverted way. A person whose dominant Function is extraverted intuition (EN) uses intuition very differently from someone who tends towards introverted intuition (IN).

The personality types

ATTITUDES	
Extraversion – e Draws energy from action Acts first, reflects, then acts again Motivation tends to decline	**Introversion – i** Energy drops during actions Prefers to reflect, then act, then reflect

Flow of energy directed outwards towards others

Action-oriented and prefers dealing with a broad range of issues

Prefers frequent interaction with others

Needs time out to reflect and re-energize

Flow of energy directed inwards towards concepts and ideas

Prefers in-depth thinking

Prefers substantial, meaningful interaction with others

PERCEIVING FUNCTIONS – INFORMATION GATHERING

Sensing – s	**Intuition – n**
Likely to trust information that is present and tangible	Trusts data that is abstract or theoretical
Tends to distrust baseless hunches	More interested in possibilities
Prefers details and facts – believing meaning is in data	Tends to trust flashes of insight
	Believes meaning lies in how the data fits patterns and theories

JUDGING FUNCTIONS – MAKING DECISIONS

Thinking – t	**Feeling – f**
Tends to take a detached approach to making decisions	Makes decisions through association and empathy
Measures decisions against a given set of rules and by what is reasonable, logical, causal and consistent	Sees problems from the inside, and seeks a solution that considers those involved and is consensual and harmonious

LIFESTYLE – RELATING TO THE OUTSIDE WORLD

Judgement – j	**Perceieving – p**
Prefers certainty and having matters settled	A preference for keeping decisions open and flexible
Indicates how they show others which Judging Function they tend towards –Thinking or Feeling:	Indicates how they show others which Perceiving Function they tend towards – Sensing or Intuition (N):
• TJ types appear logical	• SP types appear concrete
• FJ types appear empathetic	• NP types appear more abstract

THE JOHARI WINDOW

Developing yourself and strengthening teams

Developed by Joseph Luft and Harry Ingham, the Johari Window assigns aspects of personality to four 'window panes'. Each pane represents the parts of our personality that are either known or unknown to ourselves or others. Its purpose is to improve self-awareness by clarifying what we know about ourselves and discovering how we appear to others and to act as a measure of relationships and how a team is functioning.

How it works

Include descriptions about yourself in each quadrant (characteristics, behaviours, beliefs, capabilities) and ask others to compile lists of descriptions of you – add these to each window pane. The aim is to reduce aspects we hide from others and become aware of traits we're blind to, to improve our self-awareness and build stronger teams and effective relationships.

	Being open *Things I know and like others to know*.	**Blind spots** *Things others know but I do not*
Known to others	This reveals aspects that you are aware of and like others to know about. It is how you like to project yourself and how you manage your reputation, self-worth and ego. Members of strong, established teams are more open, fewer traits are hidden and work well together. Aim: to move aspects from other quadrants into this one because people work effectively in open, honest, co-operative, trusting teams.	This reveals aspects you are not aware of but that others notice. Knowing how you appear to others improves your self-awareness and enables you to explore your behaviour. Team members do not work well together when there are blind spots because it causes friction and resentment. Although comments can be difficult to hear, they will help to build better relationships.
	The hidden self *Things I know but conceal from others*	**The unknown self** *Things neither I nor others know*
Not known to others	This reveals aspects that you are aware of but prefer to conceal. Being aware of these traits (and reasons for concealment) improves self-awareness, relationships and the need to take action – to build trust, improve relationships and create positive, blame-free environments. Teams work better when hidden traits are revealed and discussed, enabling people to communicate and work together, free of mistrust and misunderstanding. Fundamentally, have a culture where individuals are not afraid to be open and honest.	Given that these are things not consciously known, this is difficult. Look deeply and reflectively by yourself or with others (such as a coach) to reveal deeper truths, motivations, beliefs and issues. Moving these from the subconscious to the conscious enables you to deal with issues and move forward. Moving these issues into the open pane, depends on their nature – some things are personal and of no relevance to business. To reveal hidden talents, try new activities or courses. Companies should provide opportunities for individuals to discover new talents and encourage people to try new things, take risks and achieve their full potential.

DOUBLE-LOOP LEARNING

Developing organizational learning

Double-loop learning is a way to break people out of a cycle that just perpetuates the way things are done. Double-loop learning encourages critical reflection of an issue, enabling people to question what underpins accepted methods, thinking and processes. Quite simply, it encourages people to ask why something is the way it is.

Overview

Organizational learning matters for many reasons. In particular, it supports successful and relevant problem solving and decision-making, avoiding slow responses and stagnation and ensuring the long-term profitability of a company. To help organizations improve how they learn, Chris Argyris and Donald Schön distinguished between single-loop and double-loop learning. Single-loop learning simply maintains and improves an existing process – it doesn't question the validity of the process. Double-loop learning involves challenging the existence and function of a process, enabling a step-change in how a company operates.

Instead of simply measuring what people do, double-loop learning is about looking at what they do not do and then changing methods, behaviour and thinking accordingly. Fundamentally, it is about challenging the status quo, testing how people both learn and apply that learning and then encouraging the adoption of a more critical approach to making improvements across a wide range of activities – from processes and plans to goals and values.

The key point of double-loop learning is that it encourages people to raise their sights from the mundane and accepted, freeing them from the constraints of existing business dogma, encouraging them to see the bigger picture and refocusing their thinking towards how to achieve even greater advances. This enables them to assess situations and problem-solve effectively and creatively to produce ideas that are more likely to lead to the right changes and deliver significant success.

Organizational learning

Single-loop learning	Tackles an issue by observing results, evaluating the situation within the current, accepted approach and devising solutions that operate within these boundaries. It seeks to improve by simply doing something better.
Double-loop learning	Considers an issue through critical reflection, challenging assumptions and thinking creatively. This type of organizational learning aims to make significant improvements through identifying the fundamental changes that are necessary to gain competitive advantage.

Following on from double-loop learning, William Isaacs advocates triple-loop learning, where people need to be constantly aware of how their language and behaviour influences the thinking and assumptions of everyone else in the company, to avoid perpetuating erroneous thinking and methods and to create the right culture and mindset.

HERON'S SIX CATEGORIES OF INTERVENTION

How to help others achieve more

Developed by the psychologist John Heron, this model identifies six different approaches to helping someone during coaching, training or development sessions. Which approach is used depends on the person, the situation and their goals, and success requires the flexibility to deploy the right style at the right moment. The model can be applied to many situations where you want to offer support, guidance or feedback.

Using the categories

These are Heron's Six Categories of Intervention:

1 Prescriptive
2 Informative
3 Confrontational
4 Cathartic
5 Catalytic
6 Supportive

It is not enough to want to help people overcome difficulties or face challenging situations; what matters is knowing how best to help each particular person. And that depends on knowing which style to use at the right time. The first three categories are authoritative, where the aim is largely to provide information and to direct the person to a particular solution. The last three aim to build people's self-confidence and to encourage them to find their own solutions. While you will sometimes need to adapt your style during a conversation, it is important to plan ahead and think about what style will be most helpful.

Category	Style	Type of comment/ question
Prescriptive	Offering advice and directing the individual	'You need to consider …' 'It would be useful to …'
Informative	Giving useful information or instructions to help with a situation and guiding the person to a solution	'This happens because …' 'The reason for that is …'
Confrontational	Being positive, confront and challenge the person to direct them to a solution or course of action	'You said this happened … but …' 'Given the situation, why did you …?'
Cathartic	Encouraging individuals to express their feelings and release built up stress, animosity and tension	'If that person was here, what would you like to say to them?' 'How did that make you feel?'
Catalytic	Adopting a reflective style to promote others to be reflective and to identify their own solutions	'How could that situation have been handled differently, and would it have made a difference?' 'What effect do you think that approach had?'
Supportive	Being empathetic to establish rapport, convey that you are on their side and build their confidence by emphasizing their achievements and capabilities	'You must have felt …' 'I can see why you …' 'You are good at …'

RECONCILING CULTURAL DIFFERENCES

Benefiting from cultural diversity

Globalization has brought many benefits and opportunities, as well as risks. One of the greatest advantages is the ability to work with new people, cultures and perspectives. Management writer Fons Trompenaars highlights several principles to ensure success.

Managing cross-cultural relationships involves three stages:

1 Being aware of the origins, nature and influence of cultural differences
2. Respecting cultural differences in style and approach
3 Reconciling cultural differences by showing people how to use a variety of values and approaches.

Universalism versus particularism

- For **universalists**, rules and procedures are applied consistently.
- For **particularists**, relationships and flexibility are more important.

Universalists assume that certain standards are right and attempt to change attitudes to match their own. Particularist societies are characterized by the bonds of relationships rather than rules.

Individualism versus communitarianism

Individualist cultures (such as Israel, Canada and the USA) are self-oriented, emphasizing individual freedom and responsibility. Communitarian cultures (such as Mexico, India and Japan) emphasize the group and common goals.

Neutral versus affective

This focuses on the extent to which people display emotions and the interaction between reason and emotion in relationships. In neutral cultures, people are taught that it is incorrect to display emotion. In affective cultures, people express their emotions.

Specific versus diffuse

This affects the way people approach situations and their involvement in relationships. People from 'specific'-oriented cultures consider each element of a situation, analysing parts separately before putting them back together.

People from 'specific'-oriented cultures separate work from personal relationships. In 'diffuse'-oriented cultures people see elements as part of a bigger picture with individualism subsumed. Examples of diffuse societies include China, Nigeria and Kuwait.

Achievement versus ascription

This focuses on how personal status is assigned. Achieved status (as found in, for example, the USA, Australia and Canada) relates to an individual's actions, whereas ascribed status (as found in, for example, Egypt, Argentina and the Czech Republic) is concerned with who you are.

Sequential versus synchronic

This is about perceptions of time. People in sequential cultures view time as a series of events, taking time and schedules seriously. Synchronic cultures view past, present and future as interrelated and do several things at once.

Internal versus external control

This has to do with the extent to which people believe that they're in control or are affected by their environment. People who have an internally controlled view believe that they dominate their environment. Those with an externally controlled view focus on their environment rather than themselves.

Reconcile differences in the following ways:

- Look for opportunities and value from both perspectives.
- Define issues in terms of dilemmas or end results – what needs to be achieved – instead of focusing on the means. Find ways to avoid compromise as this is often the lowest common denominator.
- Reach out to colleagues of different orientations. Their perspectives and experiences are potentially interesting and advantageous.
- Be willing to invest effort in communicating across cultural boundaries.
- Respect and practise generic and local business customs.

THE STRATEGIC HRM MODEL

Connecting HR with business strategy

The Human Resources Management (HRM) model integrates human resource plans directly into business strategy.

While assuming some aspects of corporate life as given, such as employee buy-in and effective team work, the HRM model serves to encourage you to gather the facts, focus your thinking, illuminate insightful information, examine the situation and develop HR solutions. The use of the model depends on how committed those involved are in following through on its findings and, more crucially, on how well the priorities of HR are already synced with the wider strategic aims of the company.

1 Preparation

Set the scene ... Make sure senior management and leaders are on board and open to change, and establish the HR review team.

2 Analyse your current and future HR profile

Look at all the various factors as they are and what you'd like them to be, including working practices, organizational and HR structure, compliance issues and culture. Always include hard data – if you're not dealing with facts, your findings and recommendations will be flawed.

Importantly, identify the gaps between what you have and what you need.

3 Identify the main HR issues

Given the gap between the current situation and the company's strategic goals, decide the key HR issues involved in achieving goals – these range from seeking cultural change and downsizing to acquiring highly skilled personnel and stronger leadership.

4 Develop an organization plan for HR

Divide your plan into four sections: people, processes, organization and technology. Review each aspect and develop an HR plan that meets the company's strategic aims.

5 Devise a plan for implementation

Prioritize the needs and detail how the plan will be achieved and who will be responsible for each aspect of implementation.

6 Implement your plan

Monitor and review progress – adjust your plan where necessary.

Most importantly, win hearts and minds and support your people. Your plans will be for nothing if you don't win people over and help them during the process of change.

HOFSTEDE'S CULTURAL DIMENSIONS

Working across borders

Geert Hofstede's model identifies five important dimensions of cultural differences that companies need to address when they operate internationally. When working with people from different countries, understanding the cultural differences will facilitate a more successful and effective relationship.

Overview

Companies often operate in a multicultural environment and Hofstede's model is used to improve the ability to work successfully across different countries. It helps people to recognize and understand the behaviour and approaches of people from different cultures and, in turn, to appreciate how their own behaviours and actions are likely to be interpreted. Originally four, a fifth dimension was added later. These are shown in this diagram.

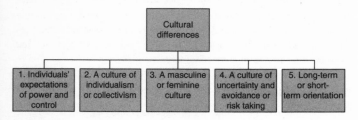

1 Individuals' expectations of power and control

Referred to as the Power Distance Index, this indicates the amount of power that people operating at the same level expect to have. People at similar levels but working in different countries will have very different expectations of how much control and power they expect to have. In some cultures, employees at a lower level will not expect much power because they operate in highly centralized and hierarchical systems. In other countries, employees at the same lower level will expect to have more power and control.

2 A culture of individualism or collectivism

A general culture of individualism or collectivism can pervade a particular country. Knowing this will help you to deal appropriately and effectively with the people involved.

3 A masculine or feminine culture

This refers to a country's general approach, values and style. For example, in masculine countries, dominance, assertiveness and ambition are all emphasized while, in feminine countries, relationship building, nurturing and supporting are highly valued.

4 A culture of uncertainly and avoidance or risk taking

Some cultures are characterized by risk aversion. These will often have regulations and practices in place to protect people against uncertainty – providing them with a higher degree of security. Conversely, some countries thrive on risk taking. This obviously has huge implications for setting and implementing strategy and for conditions of employment.

5 Long-term or short-term orientation

It is important to know whether the people in a country tend to focus on the future or on the immediate. Their values and priorities may be at odds with colleagues from different countries.

Hofstede's model of cultural dimensions is a useful reminder to be aware of differences and to plan accordingly when operating in multicultural environments. However, as with all models that focus on generalities, care should be taken as people are individuals and can have values, approaches and expectations that are different from their country's average.

ECOSYSTEMS, PARADIGMS AND THE CULTURE WEB

Understanding and managing the culture of your team or organization

Organizations can be viewed as a system of mutually reinforcing resources – an ecosystem. Closely related to the ecosystem is another factor affecting a firm's success: its cultural paradigm. When people join an organization they are taught that 'this is the way we do things'. Understanding this paradigm is enhanced using a culture web.

Cultural ecosystems

Culture is collective and learned. It keeps organizations rooted in past methods and shapes behaviour – which is why understanding culture is important to changing behaviour or implementing new strategies. Culture can change in two ways: through incremental evolution or revolution. Sometimes, when the culture is out of line with the needs of the market, a radical break with the past is needed.

What is required is an emphasis on managing value drivers (aspects that make the greatest difference and provide most benefit to customers). Of these value drivers, employee-related factors (such as employee retention, satisfaction and productivity) determine customer service, revenue growth and profitability.

Paradigms

A paradigm can be defined as the beliefs and assumptions that employees hold about an organization and take for granted. This is an inevitable feature of working in organizations – people make assumptions. They are positive when they are used to define an organization's competencies and formula for success, successfully guiding the way people work as well as allowing the organization to develop. If the paradigm is mismanaged, however, it will act as a conservative influence and a barrier to progress, adaptability and change. A valuable technique for managing paradigms is to be explicit about them, discussing their key elements and mapping them in a culture web.

The culture web

An organization's culture or paradigm is best understood through a culture web. The central paradigm is comprised of several interrelated elements:

- Stories and myths are tales (some real, some imagined) that symbolize what the organization is about.
- Symbols include logos, titles and terminology that best capture the way people work.
- Power structures are closely associated with the central paradigm and include powerful managerial groups (such as directors and the board) as well as groups that make the most money or create the brand.
- Organizational structure, which is often changed and may be easy to change, is an important aspect of the culture web. It includes formal ways of working, it reflects the power structures and it signals what is important in the organization.
- Control systems include any aspect of the organization that enables it to exert control. This includes remuneration, measurement and reward systems that indicate what behaviours are important in the organization.
- Rituals are best described as 'the way we do things here'. Often taken for granted, they include links within the organization and any activities that reflect its nature and character.

The paradigm should reflect both the ecosystem and the sources of internal competitive advantage – for example, the tacit knowledge and experience of employees should be reflected in the paradigm.

THE COMPONENTS OF CULTURE

Understanding how organizations think, behave and develop

An organization's culture can be defined as: 'the patterns of behaviour that are encouraged or discouraged by people and systems over time'. Understanding the components of culture is essential for them to be managed effectively.

Overview

An organization's culture is largely shaped by four factors: its systems, symbols, behaviours and beliefs.

- **Systems** are the way that people are supported. They include: planning and budgeting; performance review and reward; measurement and reporting; and learning and structure.
- **Symbols** are about the way resources are allocated and include issues such as: how time is spent; people promotions and exits; as well as offices, car parks and titles.
- **Behaviours** are the things that people do. They include: what is role modelled; meetings and conferences; and emails and other interactions with others.
- **Beliefs** are the intangible views, perceptions, stories, myths and legends that permeate the organization and fundamentally affect the depth, speed and quality of thinking, decisions and effort.

Six tools for managing organizational culture

There are six tools or levers to use to shape an organization's culture:

1 **Vision** – a clear, compelling view of the organization's purpose and how it will prosper. This guides the way people work.
2 **Values** – the mindset and behaviour that characterize the way people work.

3 **Practices** – how the values of an organization are translated into how it acts.
4 **People** – the personalities, priorities, experiences and attitudes of the individuals who build and sustain the culture.
5 **Narrative** – the story of the business: the heritage, successes and legends that shape people's perceptions and affect their levels of engagement, excitement and action.
6 **Place** – where people work, their physical environment and equipment, which can significantly affect the values and behaviours of people in the organization.

MANAGING CROSS-CULTURAL RELATIONSHIPS

Working successfully with people from different cultures

The best organizations recognize that, in a world where standardization and processes dominate, it is the combination of different people and the fusion of different ideas that generates progress and promotes success.

The best businesses reach out to customers and employees, managing and valuing cross-cultural relationships and ensuring maximum productivity, innovation and sales. Cultural diversity can be a valuable differentiator, enabling organizations to attract and retain the best people and helping them achieve their full potential.

Managing cross-cultural relationships is achieved by making decisions based on merit, encouraging different perspectives and challenging those behaviours that undermine other cultural or gender groups. It also means developing attitudes, practices and procedures that provide genuine equality of treatment and opportunity for all employees. Several specific techniques are particularly valuable.

Prepare for working across cultures

Broaden and develop your perspective by considering the following:

- Your own culture is unique. When working across borders you are the stranger.
- The culture you ignore most is your own. Look at yourself from the outside: What do others think?
- Others think and act differently from you.
- While your behaviour needs to adapt to norms, expectations and local customs, this does not mean imitating.

Be patient

Accept that your concept of time may be different – time frames may not be shared.

Beware of the 'denial of difference' and 'illusion of similarity'

People may be excessively polite as a way of denying difference. Statements such as 'We share the same language … we are united by the same industry, business or values' can hide a desire to avoid confronting the reality of cultural differences. Denying difference matters because it means we achieve only the lowest common denominator.

Take care when making jokes

Some jokes not only fail to travel across cultures, but they also cause offence. Humour can be a great support in cross-cultural situations but can also be culturally insensitive.

Understand each individual

Check your views and assumptions with others and:

- recognize that you may hold stereotypical views
- accept that cultural factors are mistakenly attributed to both sides
- understand motives behind a specific behaviour. Don't superficially judge behaviours against your own standards.

Reconcile differences

Resolve cultural differences by doing the following:

- Look for opportunities and the value of both perspectives, rather than favouring one or the other or seeing conflicts between different values.
- Define issues in terms of dilemmas or end results – what it is that needs to be achieved – instead of focusing on the means. Find ways to avoid compromise as this is often simply the lowest common denominator.
- Reach out to colleagues of different orientations. Their different perspectives and experiences are potentially interesting and a valuable advantage.
- Be willing to invest effort communicating across cultural boundaries.
- Respect and practise generic and local business customs, especially when it comes to communication.

THE EIGHT PRECONDITIONS FOR DIVERSITY

Diversity and competitive advantage

In a world where standardization and homogeneity dominate, diversity provides a distinctive source of competitive advantage: Eight preconditions are necessary for a business or team to benefit from identity-group differences.

Overview

Diversity is about understanding and respecting the different perspectives of our employees and customers, and it is a vital issue for a variety of commercial reasons. For example, we know that differences between people contribute significantly to making our businesses more innovative. This is not simply about visible differences such as gender, ethnicity, disability or age: it is about different perspectives on working and leadership, decision-making, managing relationships, innovating and growing our businesses.

Diversity matters because it helps us to keep pace with social and demographic change. It is a diverse world, and to be successful our business needs to reflect that diversity. Understanding and valuing diversity also helps ensure compliance with legal requirements. Finally, a positive approach to diversity matters because it is what our employees want: they feel valued and make better contributions as a result.

The eight preconditions for diversity

1 Leaders must genuinely value variety of insight and opinion.
2 Leaders must be consistent and persevere when encouraging diversity.
3 High standards of performance must be expected from everyone.
4 The leader needs to ensure that the working environment stimulates, encourages and supports personal development.

5 The leader needs to encourage openness, with a high tolerance for debate.

6 The team climate (culture) must make people feel valued and keen to contribute.

7 The vision for the team must be clear, compelling and, crucially, practical – informing and guiding behaviour.

8 The team needs to be egalitarian and non-bureaucratic – this helps people exchange ideas and value constructive challenges to the usual way of doing things.

PETER SENGE'S FIFTH DISCIPLINE

Creating a learning organization

If companies are to succeed and achieve more during times of volatility, opportunity and change, they need to be learning organizations where everyone and every function are encouraged and supported to continually adapt and improve.

Overview

Peter Senge proposed that organizations need to become learning organizations, where the full abilities of their people are harnessed to propel the company to achieve more and go further. A learning organization ensures that all aspects of a company – its people, processes and operations – are able to continually learn and adapt and are working together towards the same goal. Underpinning the learning organization is a culture of creativity: to think bigger, to think bolder, to think outside the box and, importantly, to know you can make it happen. To do this, companies need to address five areas (disciplines):

1 Systems thinking
2 Personal mastery
3 Mental models
4 Building a shared vision
5 Team learning

Each discipline is looked at from three perspectives. For each discipline, ask:

• What is the essence of what is hoped for?
• What are the principles that should guide this aspect?
• What are the practices that need to occur to make it happen?

Your people's ability to question, challenge and create depends on the environment, processes and expectations within which they work. By creating the right environment, culture and systems, your company will respond to change more quickly, instigate new market standards and become the dominant player – in short, you'll outdo the competition.

1 Systems thinking

Integrate all parts of the company – ensure that everyone and all processes are synced and are capable of continual learning and creating new possibilities. Systems thinking brings all the disciplines together and, for this reason, is considered the essence of a learning organization.

2 Personal mastery

The success of an organization depends completely on enabling and empowering its people to learn, challenge and create.

3 Mental models

Mental models are the way we interpret the world around us and condition how we behave and react. While these models can be useful, we should not be constrained by them. True progress can only be made when we are liberated from following ingrained models and are free to explore options.

4 Building a shared vision

A shared vision gains commitment and motivates people to work well together and to think bigger. It guides people's thinking, provides a rallying point for everyone in the business, and profoundly affects their decision-making. It's as simple as that.

5 Team learning

Building creative and effective teams draws on many skills. Everyone should be working and learning together towards the same goals. By sharing knowledge and ideas, we learn more as a group than we would as individuals. Consequently, when companies ensure great teamworking, they are far more likely to be market leaders.

At the core of Senge's Fifth Discipline is creation: it is not enough to be reactive; success requires us to be *proactive*.

Bibliography

Adair, John, *Action-Centred Leadership* (Gower, 1979)

Ansoff, H. Igor, *The Igor Ansof Anthology*, ed. Peter H. Antoniou and Patrick E. Sullivan (Book Surge Publishing, 2006)

Belbin, R. Meredith, *Management Teams*, 3rd edn (Routledge, 2010)

Bibb, Sally and Jeremy Kourdi, *A Question of Trust: The Crucial Nature of Trust in Business, Work & Life – and How to Build It* (Marshall Cavendish, 2006)

Blanchard, Kenneth and Spencer Johnson, *The One Minute Manager: Increase Productivity, Profits and Your Own Prosperity*, new edn (Harper, 2011)

Bono, Edward de, *Lateral Thinking: A Textbook of Creativity* (Penguin, 2009)

Bono, Edward de, *Six Thinking Hats* (Penguin, 2009)

Capodagli, Bill and Lynn Jackson, *The Disney Way Fieldbook: How to Implement Walt Disney's Vision of 'Dream, Believe, Dare, Do' in Your Own Company* (McGraw-Hill Professional, 2000)

Charan, Ram, Stephen Drotter and James Noel, *The Leadership Pipeline (How to Build the Leadership Powered Company)* (John Wiley & Sons, 2011)

Covey, Stephen R., *The Seven Habits of Highly Effective People: Powerful Lessons in Personal Change*, repr. edn (Simon & Schuster, 2004)

Curry, Jay, *Know Your Customers: How Customer Marketing Can Increase Profits* (Kogan Page, 1992)

Davies, Jacqueline and Jeremy Kourdi, *The Truth about Talent* (John Wiley and Sons, 2010)

Drucker, Peter F., *The Essential Drucker*, 2nd rev. edn (Routledge, 2007)

Galardo, Luis, *Brands & Rousers* (Lid Publishing, 2012)

Gladwell, Malcolm, *The Tipping Point: How Little Things Can Make a Big Difference*, new edn (Abacus, 2002)

Goleman, Daniel, *Emotional Intelligence: Why it Can Matter More Than IQ*, new edn (Bloomsbury Publishing, 1996)

Gratton, Lyndsay, *Why Some Companies Buzz with Energy and Innovation – and Others Don't* (Financial Times/Prentice Hall, 2007)

Hammer, Michael and James Champy, *Reengineering the Corporation: A Manifesto for Business Revolution*, 3rd rev. edn (Nicholas Brealey Publishing, 2001)

Hammond, John S., Ralph L. Keeney and Howard Raiffa, *Smart Choices: A Practical Guide to Making Smarter Life Decisions* (Crown Business, 2002)

Heron, John, *The Complete Facilitator's Handbook* (Kogan Page, 1999)

Hofstede, Geert, and Gert Jan Hofstede, *Cultures and Organizations: Intercultural Cooperation and Its Importance for Survival*, 3rd edn (McGraw-Hill, 2010)

IDEO: http://www.ideo.com

Imai, Masaaki, *Kaizen: The Key to Japan's Competitive Success* (McGraw-Hill, 1986)

Kaplan, Robert S. and David P. Norton, *The Balanced Scorecard: Translating Strategy into Action* (Harvard Business Review, 1996)

Kim, W. Chan and Renée Mauborgne, *Blue Ocean Strategy: How to Create Uncontested Market Space ad Make the Competition Irrelevant*, expanded edn (Harvard Business Review Press, 2015)

Kotter, John P., *Leading Change* (Harvard Business Review Press, 2012)

Kübler-Ross, Elisabeth, *On Death & Dying* (Simon & Schuster/Touchstone), 1969

Lax, David A. and James K. Sebenius, *3D Negotiation: Powerful Tools to Change the Games in Your Most Important Deals* (Harvard Business School Press, 2006)

Lewin, Kurt, *The Complete Social Scientist*, ed. Martin Gold (American Psychological Association, 1999)

Marchand, Donald A. and William J. Kettinger, *Information Orientation: The Link to Business Performance*, new edn (Oxford University Press, 2002)

McCarthy, Jerome E., *Basic Marketing: A Managerial Approach.* (Richard D. Irwin, 1960)

Porter, Michael E., *Competitive Advantage: Creating and Sustaining Superior Performance*, new edn (Free Press, 2004).

Porter, Michael E., *Competitive Strategy: Technique for Analyzing Industries and Competitors* (Free Press, 2004).

Rappaport, Alfred, *Creating Shareholder Value*, 2nd rev. edn (Simon & Schuster, 1998)

Schwartz, Peter, *The Art of the Long View* (Bantam Doubleday, 1991)

Senge, Peter M., *The Fifth Discipline: The Art and Practice of the Learning Organization*, 2nd rev. edn (Random House Business, 2006)

Sirota, David and Douglas Klein, *The Enthusiastic Employee: How Companies Can Benefit by Giving Workers What They Want*, 2nd edn (Pearson FT Press, 2014)

Sull, Donald N., *Why Good Companies Go Bad and How Great Managers Can Remake Them* (Harvard Business School Press, 2005)

Thomas–Kilmann Conflict Mode Instrument (Xicom, 1974)

Warren, Kim, *Building Strategy & Performance through Time: The Critical Path* (Business Expert, 2009)

Waterman, Jr., Robert H. and Tom Peters, *In Search of Excellence: Lessons from America's Best-run Companies*, 2nd edn (Profile Books, 2004)

Whitmore, Sir John *Coaching for Performance: GROWing Human Potential and Purpose: The Principles and Practice of Coaching and Leadership. People Skills for Professionals*, 4th edn (Nicholas Brealey Publishing, 2009)